Cast Me Out If You Will

Cast Me Out If You Will
Stories and Memoir

Lalithambika Antherjanam

Translated, Edited, and Introduced by
GITA KRISHNANKUTTY

Foreword by Meena Alexander

The Feminist Press
at the City University of New York

Published in the United States and Canada by
THE FEMINIST PRESS at The City University of New York
City College/CUNY, Wingate Building, Convent Avenue at 138 Street
New York, NY 10031

Published simultaneously in India by STREE, an imprint of
Bhatkal & Sen, 16 Southern Avenue, Calcutta 700 026.
Published in the United States and Canada
by arrangement with Stree.

First U.S. edition, 1998

Library of Congress Cataloging-in-Publication Data
ANTHERJANAM, LALITHAMBIKA, 1909–1985
    Cast Me Out If You Will : stories and memoir/
    Lalithambika Antherjanam; translated, edited, and
    introduced by Gita Krishnankutty; foreword by Meena
    Alexander. — 1st ed.
        p.   cm.
Translated from the Malayalam.
Includes bibliographical references.
        ISBN 1-55861-187-8
        ISBN 1-55861-188-6 (pbk.)
    1. Indic literature—Translations into English. 2. Indic
literature (English)—20th century—History and criticism. 3.
Women in literature. I. Krishnankutty, Gita. II. Title.
PR9484.6.l36 1998
891/.1 21   97-32979
                                                                   CIP

The Feminist Press would like to thank Joanne Markell and
Genevieve Vaughan for their generosity in supporting this publication

Typesetting and design by Compuset International, Calcutta, and
printed by Gopsons Papers Pvt. Ltd., A-28, Sector IX, Noida, U.P., India

05 04 03 02 01 00 99 98   5 4 3 2 1

For my mother,
who taught me even when I did not want to learn

G. K.

Acknowledgments

I would like to thank all those who helped me generously during the time I worked on this collection. First of all, N. Mohanan very kindly agreed to let me undertake the English translation of the stories and memoir by his mother, Lalithambika Antherjanam. I am grateful to Susie Tharu for her unfailing encouragement and help.

I was fortunate that Lakshmi Holmstrom and Usha Aroor took an interest in the earliest drafts and gave valuable suggestions. I would like to thank everyone at the Vanikalebaram Vayanasala, Chengamanad, especially C. R. Ramachandran, for their help with books and background material. I am grateful to Kuttikrishna Variar, K. A. Sharma and Purushothaman Namboodiri, all of Chengamanad, for elucidating innumerable details in the text, to Malini Marar for answering my frantic last minute queries and to Vijaya Vanamala, Jayasri Kalathil and P. Madhavan, all of Hyderabad, for generous assistance with the proofs.

G . K.

Contents

Foreword

HOMELESS VOICES

IN HER SHORT STORY "The Goddess of Revenge," Lalithambika Antherjanam paints a vivid portrait of a woman writer. It is an image that resonates for us here, now.

The writer is alone in her room, and like so many parents she first checks to see that her children are asleep before she turns to her labors. She knows she needs to complete the task of writing, but the actual stuff, the material of her art, is not revealed to her: "I had to finish writing today, come what may, but what was I going to write about? How was I to begin?" The question is far from innocuous. It pierces to the very heart of her enterprise.

For even to think of what she might write is to bring on anger at the recrimination aimed at her as a writer. To publish what she wrote was to face the scorn of a world that kept women in seclusion—to tempt fate in a way that only the boldest or the most desperate would do. As a woman of the Namboodiri brahmin caste in Travancore, in the early twentieth century, Lalithambika was born into a world of stricture and decorum that forced her to keep herself in ritual seclusion. Yet as a writer she had to reveal the truth of her heart. Hence the poignant words in the memoir piece "Sesame Seeds, Flowers, Water," where she addresses her dead mother—a mother to whom she never showed any of her writings "because I was convinced I was doing something wrong." This wrongdoing lies at the very quick of her life: "I put them [my memories] down here, Amme, as they spill out of my mind—for your daughter has this unfortunate habit of wanting to record everything she thinks and feels, since she happens to be a writer."

Being a writer means telling the intimate truth of a life, and for Lalithambika, the exhilaration of the act, part of her psychic survival, still required braving the punishment of home and world. Clearly the vitality of the nationalist movement in India permitted many women of Lalithambika's generation to enter into the turmoil of the public realm, but the anticolonial struggle, even as it energized the struggle for women's rights, could in no way annul the pain of a silenced femininity. Out of this silence came buried voices.

In the story "The Goddess of Revenge," told by a woman writer, distress at the imagined response of her readers, even as it forces her eyes shut, fills the narrator's spirit with voices of the living and dead: "creatures tormented by pain, those who had lost their voices. . . . Were they demanding to be transcribed?" And it is quite precisely these homeless voices—these "invisible presences," to use Virginia Woolf's phrase—that bring the woman writer to her art.

When a delicate voice questions her, we realize that the writer is face to face with her muse, the Other who, holding up a mirror, coaxes her forward, through the kingdom of fear. But Tatri—the woman cast out by Namboodiri society, confronting its punishing statutes, her whole body "explosive" at the "heart of a great silence"—is also the muse who is split by a terrible ambivalence, haunted by the sense of having "fallen." Even as she can revolt, witness, and tell, there is no escape from history.

The ritual displacement of women in traditional Namboodiri society forms the core of Lalithambika's work and stands at the heart of her powerful novel *Agnisakshi* (Trial by Fire). In the novel and in some of the short stories included in this volume, the self doubles, splits into two: the self that endures, mute, voiceless, and the other self that bears witness, taking on the role of writer or narrator. What else is there to do? Where else can the woman writer turn? In the struggle with the prescriptions of an all-powerful culture, her own bodily self—passionate, desiring, violated, silenced—becomes the very ground of speech. I have called this, elsewhere in my writing on Lalithambika, a "back against the wall aesthetic," a recourse to the most primitive ground: the body as the site of first and last resort. In an art that comes out of the conditions of oppression, the female body—marked up, written over, bound into ritual seclusion—becomes itself the instrument of freedom.

In her lyrical memoir piece "Childhood Memories" Lalithambika speaks of the great house, the *tarawad*, into which she was born; of her father's discomfort at the social prescriptions that could force him to forget that girls were also human beings; of the rich nurture her parents gave her when she was a small child, feeding her food, stories, newspapers, books. She describes how as a child she wrote with an ostrich feather and how she made her own ink by mixing ground kadukka nuts, copper sulfate, and sometimes the petals of the hibiscus flower. But puberty becomes cause for fear. This girlchild must "die"—all her activity must cease. If this is not a literal death, it is one almost as fierce, for it becomes the prelude to her seclusion, her confinement in the *antahpuram*, the women's quarters of the house.

In the two years she spends in seclusion Lalithambika gains what she calls her "real education." The "unfortunate souls" of countless women, their homeless voices, enter into her. The terrible injustice in how their fate is decided fires her to write. But the writing she does, even as it is inspired in part by the great Bengali writer Tagore, causes a painful self-division. She reads what she writes, weeps, tears up the pages. In a moral education as fierce as the one that Mary Wollstonecraft put herself through, this Kerala woman writer enters the molten terrain of feminism. All that was already given—the strictures of family, caste, creed, and even Indian nationalism, the new promise of her generation—had to be questioned, stripped apart in the quest for truth. But if pain could not be avoided, what Lalithambika Antherjanam gives us is the possibility of a world rewritten, risen up out of injustice.

In my early years in America I wrote a poem set in Kerala, home of my ancestors. In it I imagine a traditional house and a woman of my grandmother's generation whose "debt is endless"—a debt acquired not because of anything she has done, but because of what she is, in her woman's flesh. She can neither enter the house into which she has been married, nor can she leave it. She kneels perpetually at the threshold. There is no other posture for her. What Lalithambika Antherjanam has given me, given all of us, is passage through that world.

HOUSE OF A THOUSAND DOORS

This house has a thousand doors
the sills are cut in bronze
three feet high
to keep out snakes
toads, water rats
that shimmer in the bald reeds
at twilight
as the sun burns down to the Kerala coast.

The roof is tiled in red
pitched with a silver lightning rod,
a prow, set out from land's end
bound nowhere.
In dreams
waves lilt, a silken fan
in grandmother's hands.

She kneels at each
of the thousand doors in turn
paying her dues.
Her debt is endless.
I hear the flute played in darkness,
a bride's music.
A poor forked thing,
I watch her kneel in all my lifetime
imploring the household gods
who will not let her in.

New York 1997   MEENA ALEXANDER

NOTES

For further thoughts on Lalithambika Antherjanam's novel *Agnisakshi* see Meena Alexander, "Skin with Fire Inside: Indian Women Writers," in *The Shock of Arrival: Reflections on Postcolonial Experience* (Boston: South End Press, 1996.) The poem was first printed in *House of a Thousand Doors* (Washington DC: Three Continents Press, 1988.)

Introduction

A N ENCHANTED CHILDHOOD, spent roaming the countryside, swimming, boating, and playing on the lush hillsides surrounding her home, came to an abrupt end the day Lalithambika reached puberty. When she writes about her early years as a joyful, carefree child, there is no mistaking her nostalgia and sorrow. At fifteen she became "a caged bird in her fortress home" (she puns on the name of her family's home, Kottavattath, which means "the circle of the fortress"), a prisoner, denied the right to go anywhere, or to meet people, or even to sit in the front room and listen while her father and his friends discussed the stirring events taking place in the country.

Lalithambika Antherjanam was born on 30 March 1909, in a namboodiri *illam* in what was at that time the state of Travancore. The namboodiris were a relatively small community of Kerala brahmins. Namboodiri women were known as *anterjanams*, which translates as "those who live inside." As wealthy priests and landowners, namboodiris exercised enormous cultural and economic authority. During the years Lalithambika was growing up, movements concerned about the oppressions of the caste system and the sufferings of women had begun to gather force in this southern region. But namboodiri girls remained largely untouched by those impulses; they continued to live very restricted lives, and the little freedom they enjoyed as young children was never to recur. Once they reached puberty, they were regarded as *asuryampasyakal*, literally, those who should never see the sun. They were confined to their homes and had to observe the namboodiri rules of seclusion. If they had to go out, they were required to shield their faces with palm-leaf umbrellas, cover themselves entirely with a shawl of unbleached cloth, and leave in the company of a female chaperone. The namboodiris were in fact renowned for their orthodoxy and their resistance to change. Unlike many other communities in Kerala, such as the nairs, the ezhavas, or the Syrian Christians, the namboodiris resisted the Western influences that came with colonialism in the nineteenth century and were most reluctant to respond to the reform movements that swept through Kerala in the early twentieth century.

Of the sixty-four *anacharams*, which were practices that were to be observed by the entire namboodiri community, many of which were concerned with the strict maintenance of ritual purity, some applied only to the anterjanams. These included the injunctions that women could not look at men other than their husbands; that they were not to cover the upper body when at home; that their noses could not be pierced; that they may not commit sati or shave their heads when widowed. Custom also required that anterjanams wore only white clothing, and that they had their earlobes lengthened to wear heavy dangling earrings. Clothing and body-marks were indices of caste status: to dress differently, therefore, would be to challenge the social order. The name of the sage Parasurama, who was believed to have brought the namboodiri brahmins to Kerala, was invoked to endorse these customs.

The legend holds that Parasurama, an incarnation of Vishnu, killed all the Kshatriyas, or warriors, in the land. In remorse, he made over his kingdom to holy men. Finding himself homeless, he appealed to them for a piece of land. They granted him what he could claim with a single throw of an ax. Parasurama threw his ax from Kanyakumari to Gokarnam, whereupon the sea retreated to form the strip of land that is Kerala. Parasurama then brought in a select group of brahmins, the namboodiris, to whom he gave control of the lands. Beneath them were a caste of warriors, the nairs. The ezhavas, who were agriculturists, formed a caste below the nairs. At the bottom of the hierarchy were the peasant and artisan castes (pulaya and paraya among them) who were considered untouchable. Two other relatively large communities that feature in Lalithambika's fiction are the Syrian Christians and the mapilla Muslims. Both groups trace their origins in Kerala to the early centuries A.D. when the spice trade with West Asia and North Africa was at its height.[1]

Historians have suggested that the namboodiris owe their origin to the thirty-two settlements made by brahmin families who came from the northern regions of the subcontinent in the fourth and fifth centuries A.D. Initially the namboodiris were only priests and temple trustees. Between the eighth and eleventh centuries, however, they also became the major landowning class in Kerala.[2] For several centuries they continued to wield tremendous spiritual and temporal authority. By the nineteenth century, with the rise of the nairs and the coming of colonialism, their political power began to be eroded. Yet, as is also evident in the story "The Power of Fate," as the great landholders, or *jenmis*, they continued to exercise the authority of life and death over their tenants well into the twentieth century.

Strict marriage and inheritance laws ensured that namboodiri landholdings remained consolidated. Only the eldest son, who also inherited the property, married within the community. Other sons formed *sambandhams*, or contractual relationships, mainly with the women of the matrilineal nair community. As a result, the anterjanams faced several problems. Since only an eldest son could marry within the community, it was very difficult to find husbands for namboodiri girls. Dowries were high, and the less affluent families could not afford the cost of securing a young husband marrying for the first time. Rather than risk a daughter remaining unmarried, which was unacceptable according to his religious beliefs, a namboodiri father was often willing to give her in marriage to an eldest son who was already married. Many young women were married off to eldest sons who were old, ill, or even about to die. Men of sixty could be married to young girls of twelve or thirteen. Once the husbands died, the young widows were condemned to dreary lives spent between the kitchen and the prayer room and, in many cases, to ill-treatment at the hands of older wives. It was the miserable plight of the anterjanams that gave rise to the earliest stirrings of protest against patriarchal oppression in Kerala. Consequently, those struggles—and the literature that arose around them—are founding moments and founding texts for feminism in Kerala.

Lalithambika herself was fortunate in having exceptionally enlightened parents who allowed her as much freedom as they could within the confines of the extended family. Her father, Kottavattath Damodaran Potti, was a poet deeply involved in social reform movements. Her mother, Nangayya Antherjanam, was the daughter of a well-known poet, Subramanian Potti. She had been sent to a temple school meant exclusively for brahmins. "It was unbelievable in those days that an anterjanam should go to school. Yet Nangayya Antherjanam went to a Malayalam school and completed the education available there," writes Joseph Paimbilli.[3] It is interesting that, despite her orthodox temple-school education, devotional poems that she composed while on a pilgrimage to Banares included prayers to gods of all religions.

Lalithambika was the only girl among nine children. Both her parents nurtured their daughter's desire for learning. She was taught Malayalam and Sanskrit at home and encouraged to read the books and the magazines that filled the house. In the autobiographical essay "Childhood Memories," she recalls how deeply her father resented his inability to provide her with a "proper education," to "bring her up like a human being," and how he endeavored to make up for this by ensuring that she always had enough to read. Her mother discussed books with her and introduced her to the poetry and fiction of the period. Her parents also took the risk of permitting her important concessions in the way she dressed. Her earlobes were not lengthened in the customary way and she was allowed to wear gold studs instead of cumbersome dangling earrings. She was probably the first girl in her community to wear a skirt and a blouse and not have to leave her breasts uncovered. Her parents, however, could not totally avoid imposing certain restrictions that their society insisted upon. She was therefore confined to the *antahpuram,* or the women's quarters, as soon as she began to menstruate, and she spent the years until her marriage within its limits.

Namboodiri illams of the kind that Lalithambika and her family lived in were elaborate houses set in large compounds. The main living quarters, known as the *nalukettu*, were arranged around a central sunken courtyard, open to the sky and flanked by four (or sometimes eight) wooden pillars. A veranda ran around the sides of the courtyard and rooms opened out from it. The kitchen and the room that adjoined it, the *vadikkini*, were in the northern wing of the courtyard. The women of the household spent most of their time in this wing, which was their chief area of activity. In the autobiographical piece dedicated to her mother, "Sesame Seeds, Flowers, Water," Lalithambika mentions that the distance between the kitchen and the outer room just beyond the nalukettu of her house was about a furlong, or 200 meters, and her mother had to cover it repeatedly during the course of the day while carrying out her chores. The deities were installed in the southeastern wing in a room called the *thevarappura*. Besides the main building, there were granaries, a gatehouse, sheds for pounding grain and housing cattle, and at least a couple of square tanks or ponds, one for bathing and the others for kitchen uses. A well dug alongside the kitchen wall allowed water to be drawn directly into the kitchen for cooking and for all the rituals. Scrupulous maintenance of ritual purity was imperative, especially in the kitchen and its vicinity, and women were required to observe the necessary rites carefully.

Echoes of the political and social upheavals taking place in the outside world did, however, find their way into the antahpuram where Lalithambika was confined in the years before her marriage. Her real education, she says, took place in these years. She often talks about the leaders of the reform movements in Kerala, describing them as men and women of vision and passion. The organizations founded by these people fought bravely against the oppression of women and caste hierarchies and worked actively for the spread of education. The first such group to emerge, the Sree Narayana Dharma Paripalana Yogam, was established in 1903 by Sree Narayana Guru (1855–1929), who belonged to the lower-caste ezhava community. The gulf between the so-called higher and lower castes in Kerala at this period was so colossal that an untouchable pulaya could pollute a nair if he or she transgressed the distance barrier of sixty paces. A namboodiri was polluted if a pulaya even appeared within his range of vision. Lalithambika often alludes to the teachings of Narayana Guru, who argued for "one caste, one religion, and one God," as well as those of his follower, Kumaran Asan (1873–1924), one of Kerala's greatest poets. Asan's most famous work, *Duravasta* (Tragic Plight) is set against the backdrop of the Mapilla Rebellion that took place in 1920 –1921. This rebellion was one in a long line of uprisings of peasants, mostly Muslims, directed principally against the namboodiri landlords. Asan's revolutionary story connects the women's question to the caste question since it relates the tale of a namboodiri girl who finds refuge in the home of an "untouchable" pulaya laborer.[4]

In Kerala, the late nineteenth- and early twentieth-century struggles against the oppression of women were focused mainly on the plight of the anterjanams. In 1909, the year in which Lalithambika was born, V. T. Bhattadiripad, a namboodiri angered by the ills prevalent in his community, founded the Namboodiri Yogakshema Sabha. This group established a magazine, held discussions and debates on current social problems, and advocated the spread of education. They made efforts to abolish the practice of allowing men to marry more than one wife. The more progressive members of the Yogakshema Sabha eventually formed another group, the Yuvajana Sangham, which took up more radical issues like the remarriage of widows. They continued this work over the years that the young Lalithambika was growing up and well into the thirties.

These reform movements constituted one of the two major shaping forces of Lalithambika Antherjanam's work. The other influence was the nationalist movement. In contrast to what appears to have happened in other parts of India—and notably so in Bengal, and Maharashtra, where there were major tensions and conflicts between the reform movements and the emerging nationalist movement—in Kerala social reform movements of all kinds, particularly those concerned with the removal of untouchability, became identified with the Congress-led nationalist movement and the leadership of Gandhi. Gandhi had initially lent support to the Mapilla Rebellion in Malabar and was actively involved in the conduct of the 1924–1925 Vaikkam satyagraha, demanding the right of all castes to use the roads around the Vaikkam temple.[5] Lalithambika writes about how, aged thirteen, she was inspired by a "kind of blind worship" for the activities of the Congress party, and especially Gandhi, who was at the time in jail, to write an article about them which she sent secretly to a magazine. It was her father who found it in print in an issue of *Sarada* that reached him along with the rest of his mail one day in August 1923. He was immensely pleased to have discovered his daughter as a writer and encouraged her to write more.

Lalithambika's first attempt at fiction was a novel she wrote when she was fifteen, inspired by Rabindranath Tagore's *Gharey Bairey* (The Home and the World) which she had just read in a Malayalam translation.[6] The central character in the novel is a young woman, Bimala, torn between the "safe" inner-quarters world and the perilous yet exciting outside, torn also between Sandeep, fiery leader of an early nationalist initiative to whom she is passionately drawn, and the enlightened rationality of her gentle husband, Nikhilesh. Lalithambika was charmed by the novel. Its characters, she felt, could easily be people in her own world. In "A Woman Writer Replies," she describes how she came to write a similar novel that no one but she ever saw, and that finally crumbled away to dust in an old box.

Lalithambika's marriage in 1927 changed her life. She writes that she found in her husband, Narayanan Namboodiri, an encouraging companion who always acknowledged her right to express herself fearlessly. She was now free to participate in the protest movements of her time. Her relatively secure position as the daughter of enlightened parents and wife of a supportive husband made her sensitive to the pain of others. She knew that it was only her good fortune that her life was no longer bleak. After their marriage, Narayanan and Lalithambika continued to live with her parents.

In her memoir she describes her involvement in the theatrical activities of the reform groups and the stunning effect that the plays had on her society. V. T. Bhattadiripad's *Adukkalayilninnu Arangathekku* (From the Kitchen to the Scene of Action) was first performed before the Yogakshema Sabha in 1929. It was acclaimed by young namboodiri audiences, although older and more orthodox people remained severely critical of it. In the play a young anter-janam is being forced into marriage with an old namboodiri. She is in love with a young man who also wants to marry her. But he is a younger son, and custom decrees that he may not marry. On the advice of friends in Madras, he obtains a court injunction to stop the marriage on the grounds that it is being conducted against the young woman's wishes. The young man and woman then marry, thus defying tradition. At the end of the play the bride is brought to the dais at a meeting of the Yuvajana Sangham where her husband removes her *moodupadam*, the long sheet of unbleached cloth that covered an anterjanam, and tears it to shreds. In these plays the women's parts were always taken by young men since it was unthinkable at the time for namboodiri girls to appear on the stage.

In 1930 M. R. Bhattadiripad, another writer-activist, wrote a play which became an even greater success. Audiences reportedly wept as they watched it. Called *Marakkudaykkullile Mahanarakam* (The Hell Behind the Screen of the Umbrella), the play is about a young anterjanam given in marriage to an old namboodiri. His other wives treat her so badly that she commits suicide. Lalithambika refers to the two plays in the essay "A Writer Is Born" and describes how it infuriated orthodox namboodiris to see an anterjanam without her umbrella and shawl, despite the fact that it was only a man acting the part. In 1934, Lalithambika herself wrote a play in which a young widow remarries. Although it was staged successfully many times, she refused to have it published. She discusses the circumstances in which she wrote it in "An Account of a Performance."

In 1932, Lalithambika attended a conference that was to become a major event in Kerala history, the Nair Sammelanam, organized by Mannath Padmanabhan at Mavelikkara to honor Parvathi Nenmini Mangalam and Arya Pallam. These anterjanams had cast away their umbrellas and covering shawls, repudiating the restrictions of seclusion. Lalithambika had not told her parents where she was going. When she returned without umbrella or shawl, she found an outraged family who condemned her actions. Only her father offered his silent support. The event disturbed her all the more because this was her first serious conflict with her mother. Although she shared a close bond of affection with her mother, the older woman failed to understand her daughter's commitment to the questions that were beginning to change the very nature of their society. Lalithambika pays tribute to her mother in the long essay, "Sesame Seeds, Flowers, Water," where she recalls, with infinite tenderness, their many differences of opinion as well as their deep attachment for each other.

For Lalithambika, the consequences of breaking namboodiri caste laws were severe. She was forced to leave her home. Her father built a small house for the young couple and their three small children. Lalithambika recalls the following ten years lived there as idyllic. There, they "learned to use our tools skillfully: my husband his hoe, and I my pen." They were free to live as they wished and to receive all their friends regardless of caste. Then her father died. Economic exigencies and Lalithambika's own ill health forced a move to her husband's family's conservative household, "with its innumerable inmates, its endless domestic squabbles, and its old-fashioned ways of living." As a child, the only sister of eight brothers, and as a mother of seven, Lalithambika had experienced the varied joys and irritations of life in a large extended family. But the experiences had not prepared her for the rigid, custom-dominated "corridors of darkness" of her husband's family's household. The people around her furnished her with inexhaustible material for her stories: "Crying without tears, life with no soul, rooms where no blood had been spattered, but no human beings only wraiths and shadows moved . . . their smiles no different from their tears." [7]

Judging from her fiction, what grieved her most about namboodiri society was the large number of widows and unmarried women who were incarcerated and continued to live, as one of Lalithambika's characters says, "only because they could not die." The only outings permitted were to the temples:

> Fear was the main emotion they knew. They could be accused of the most inconsequential misdoings, be tried by a special court and be cast out of society . . . The tears, the pain, the suffering of unhappy anterjanams, old spinsters, widows disowned by their families and dissatisfied co-wives, filled the antahpurams . . . [8]

Bitter and resentful, some broke down completely and were dismissed as mad or hysterical. Others took refuge in near-fanatic espousals of religion. A number of stories—"Within the Folds of Seclusion" and "The Devi and Her Devotee," among them—deal with the horrors of incarceration and with awakened sexualities denied expression.

Younger sons in a namboodiri household normally formed alliances with nair women who, being matrilineal, continued to live in their own households, but unmarried anterjanams were expected to remain virgins. If an anterjanam dared to break out of her isolation and formed a relationship with a man, or should she even be suspected of doing so, she was removed to the *anchampura*, a place that was outside the women's quarters, and tried for her "crime" by a court convened within the illam. This trial was known as the *smartavicharam*, and was conducted, in the presence of a representative of the king, by male namboodiris called *smartans* who held special legal powers. The court consisted of a smartan judge, two or more *mimamsakas* (namboodiris versed in their caste laws), the *agakoyma* or local head of the community, and the *purakoyma*, the king's representative. The trial began with the worship of the family's deity, after which a *dasi*, a woman servant, was called upon to give evidence against the accused, and also to serve as her mouthpiece, since the anterjanam herself could not be seen by those trying her. The crime was called *adukkaladosham*, literally, pollution of the kitchen. The logic was that since the ritual purity of the kitchen, crucial for maintaining the household's caste status, was in the hands of the women, it was called into question the moment a woman of the household was suspected of an illicit relationship. The trial could be spun out over months and could involve the family in an enormous expenditure, since the entire judicial committee had to be fed and housed by the family of the accused. The accused was often terrorized into confession; once found guilty, she was divested of her umbrella and the shawl, which had hitherto marked her as an anterjanam, and called a *sadhanam*, or an object. An outcast now, a *bhrashta*, she had no home or family and was expelled from the household and expected to fend for herself. The rites of the dead were performed for her.

In her autobiographical essays, Lalithambika mentions instances of several women who were accused and punished in this way, sometimes for the pettiest of crimes. One of her best-known stories, "Admission of Guilt," is the brilliant and deeply moving defence given by a young widow who is brought to the smartavicharam. "Goddess of Revenge" describes an unusual smartavicharam that took place in Kerala in 1905. Earlier, anterjanams accused of adultery had been forced to confess and were then extradited, along with the men whose guilt had been proven. In 1904, the Maharaja, Rama Varma, modified the rules to enable the accused woman to question and cross-examine her alleged partners. "Goddess of Revenge" is based on a real-life character, Kuriyedathu Tatri, who is famed for having conceived and carried out an elaborate plan of revenge. Abandoned by her namboodiri husband, Tatri became a prostitute and continued to live as one, "forgotten" by her family. The exact circumstances that precipitated the charges are not clear, but seem related to the changed laws. It is possible that Tatri herself had some hand in precipitating the trial. At the smartavicharam, Tatri herself arraigned sixty-four men who were consequently cast out of the community. Those present commented on the skill with which she performed, "like a lawyer." The trial, which made history, was widely reported throughout South India.[9] Anterjanams were forbidden to pronounce Tatri's name, apparently because she had chosen to become a prostitute. Lalithambika reconstructs the details from an account whispered to her when she was a very young girl by a half-crazed grandmother. "It was extraordinarily courageous for a twenty-eight-year-old woman to write a story like that, a half-century ago," writes the well-known critic M. Leelavathi.[10] In "Lessons from Experience," Lalithambika herself reports how she was attacked after the story appeared in 1938.

During the thirties and the forties, the demands of her growing children, the interminable household chores, and the sheer pressures of everyday living laid claim on her time and energy. Yet she managed to snatch time for her writing, mostly during the night when she sat awake after her family had fallen asleep. These two decades, from the mid-thirties to the mid-fifties, were also her most productive years. She produced several volumes of stories and, as the memoir also indicates, engaged energetically in literary and other debates. Most of her fiction first appeared in newspapers or magazines and was later collected into books brought out regularly, every three or four years between 1937, when *Adyathe Kathakal* (First Stories) was published and 1960, when *Satyathinte Swaram* (The Notes of Truth) came out.

The late thirties were also years of intense political activity in Kerala as in the rest of India. There were marches and fasts demanding the right of entry into the famous temple at Guruvayur for the so-called untouchable castes. In marches that wound their way through villages across the state, activists raised the questions of caste oppression and agrarian reform and supported strikes of factory workers, while they also lent support to the civil disobedience struggles being carried out in other parts of India.[11] The political movements grew, in numbers as well as in terms of the issues they took on, and became increasingly radical. In 1938 two major events shook the government of the princely state of Travancore. These were a massive protest march of peasants, workers, and students in support of striking workers in an Allapuzha factory, and another march of "over 20,000 people, easy," that was led by the activist Akkamma Cheriyan (1909–1982). Akkamma was at the time president of the Kerala state Congress party. The marchers confronted the seat of power in Thiruvananthapuram to demand the release of arrested activists.[12] Lalithambika herself was not directly involved in public politics—she says she "dealt with the world around her solely on the basis of information gleaned from the newspapers"—yet there is a figurative conjunction in her work between the nation struggling for independence and the woman fighting her oppression.[13] Both these themes fire her imagination. She recalls that she "wrote, read, and made speeches. When I look back, I see the young mother crouched on the ground, writing as she rocks the cradle. I see the willful, ignorant young woman, standing on a public platform, holding her baby close to her while she makes a speech . . ."[14] Lalithambika often discusses the tension between her commitments as a wife and a mother and her identity as a writer. It is evident that she worked hard to fulfill her numerous domestic obligations, even though she realized that these prevented her from giving her writing the single-minded attention it required. "A writer must read, study, think, write and engage in debate," she points out in "Lessons from Experience." She also tells us there how she managed her three jobs as family person, social reformer, and serious writer.

The themes of the thirties and the forties remained with Lalithambika for many years after India's independence in 1947. Yet, from the early fifties onward there are indications of a disillusionment that began to set in. Lalithambika was one of the many women from all walks of life who supported Akkamma Cheriyan in 1953 when she stood for election, as an independent, challenging the ruling Congress candidate. Akkamma had been one of the stalwarts of the long struggle for independence, yet much to everyone's surprise, when in 1948 the lists of ministers were drawn up for the new government, her name did not appear. In the 1952 elections the party did not even list her as a candidate. She resigned from the Congress, which she declared had fallen into the hands of opportunists. In a subsequent by-election she stood as an independent, backed by all the opposition parties and supported by thousands disillusioned with the Congress-in-government. Eight months pregnant, she ran a hectic campaign in which she also specifically addressed the large numbers of women who came to her meetings. Of the 126 candidates nominated by the Congress in 1952, not one was a woman, she said. Congress leaders had said that the only proper place for women was in the kitchen. Hence, a victory for Akkamma would be a victory for the women of Kerala. Akkamma lost the seat, though she won 43 percent of the nearly 300,000 votes cast. Lalithambika's story, "Gandhijikkushesham" (After Gandhi), not in this collection but written around this time, reflects on the issues raised by Akkamma's experiences. In the stories "'Come Back'" and "Dhirendu Majumdar's Mother" and in the novel *Agnisakshi* (Witness by Fire) we have other narratives on the nationalist movement's promises to women which criticize the outcome.

Though not a Marxist herself, Lalithambika supported the progressive movement in Malayalam literature. In 1957 she presided over the meeting held to celebrate the victory of the communist government. "Olivilninnu Olivilekku" (From Hiding Place to Hiding

Place) and "Achande Makan" (His Father's Son), both not included in this collection, indicate that she understood and valued the risks young communists were taking and that she regarded them as the sons who had really inherited the spirit of their freedom-fighter fathers. However, in "Daughter of Humanity," written after the communist government had passed the 1959 land-ceiling laws, she raises the difficult question of what happens to the women in the namboodiri households that were breaking up as a result of the laws. "She is on the side of the victim, whether a communist or a one-time landlord trapped in the process of change," M. Leelavathi concludes.[15]

In the early seventies Lalithambika began work on a set of essays based on thirteen women characters, six from the *Ramayana* and seven from the *Mahabharata*. Gently disengaging these women from the epic plots in which they are set, she probes what might have been their personal anxieties and their particular existential crises and rewrites their stories with sympathy. In *Sita Muthal Satyavathi Vare* (From Sita to Satyavathi), written in 1972, Sita emerges as "a worthy source of female power" who condemns the meanness of her husband, Ahalya as "deserving compassion rather than derision," and Dussala as the tragic victim of the avarice of her Kaurava brothers.[16]

The warmth with which Lalithambika writes in her memoir about her long friendship with her husband, and the sense of achievement she has about her own life, are both evident also in the story "Fulfillment." The story is about a couple ripened, like the fruit in their garden, and about the glow that fulfillment imparts to their very quotidian lives. She also continued, right to the very end of her life, to address meetings and engage in debates. Inaugurating a youth festival in Kottayam in 1987, a few days before her death, she once again brought together the two major themes of her life: the struggle to change society and a belief in the social responsibility of the artist. She said she could not accept the worth of art severed from life and from the love of humankind.[17] On another occasion she wrote, "If the mode of bliss, which is the ideal of pure art, were my only medium, I would have spent my life . . . writing verses to Kali or *kaikottikkali* songs. I would not have had to walk through fire to find the power of expression."[18]

Lalithambika began by writing poems. An initial collection, *Lalithanjali* (Simple Offerings) appeared in 1936. The short story, however, was her preferred form and her stories do indeed constitute her best and most important work. After her first collection, which came out in 1937, eleven more volumes appeared. The best-known among them are: *Kalathinde Edukal* (Pages from History), 1950; *Moodupadathil* (Within the Folds of Seclusion), 1946; *Koddumkattil Ninnu* (From a Whirlwind), 1951; *Irupathu Varshathinu Sesham* (Twenty Years Later), 1956; *Agnipushpangal* (Flowers of Fire), 1960; and *Dhirendu Majumdarude Amma* (Dhirendu Majumdar's Mother), 1973. Though she is less well known as a poet, she published seven collections, including a commemorative volume, *Aayirathiri* (A Thousand [Burning] Wicks), 1969. She has also written prize-winning stories for children, and a volume of much-loved traditional songs for children, *Thenthullikal* (Drops of Honey). In 1976, at the age of sixty-seven, she published her first and only novel, *Agnisakshi*. It won the Vayalar award, and the state as well as the central Sahitya Akademi awards.

The pieces chosen for translation here are selected from the short story collections and from a memoir, *Atmakathakkoru Amukkham* (Preface for an Autobiography), which appeared in 1979. In a brief foreword to the memoir, Lalithambika writes that on her seventieth birthday she decided to publish a few essays that touched on her past and on issues that deeply concerned her. Many of these pieces had first appeared in magazines; others were radio talks. She also included some pages from her diary, mostly jottings made during a visit to Kanyakumari in 1944 to rest after an illness. C.V. Kunhiraman, the founder of the influential journal *Kerala Kaumudi*, had asked her at that time to write her autobiography, but at thirty-five, she felt she had only begun her life and that experience had to be transmuted in memory before she could begin such a task. Later she realized that she had been "afraid to turn and look back into myself. I felt shy, hesitant. In short I felt the same weakness that the anterjanam of old experienced when she cast aside her moodupadam and went out. I still have some of that reluctance."[19] At seventy, she agreed that she had the maturity to reflect on the past, but lacked the necessary sharpness of memory and clarity of analysis. All the same, since time was running out, she decided to gather for publication at least a "handful of bits and pieces" written at various times.

Lalithambika comments that a life of opposition—to her family and to society—was not what she would ever have chosen for herself, but that in her time that was the only means of expression open to her. She regrets that her articles and stories are full of conflict and argument. She feels that she was forced constantly to perform a task she was untrained for and that it prevented her from serving the cause of art as she would have desired. On several occasions in the memoir as well as in interviews, Lalithambika discusses the problems faced by a woman who wants to write. In 1969, in response to a question about why women have figured so poorly in the canon of Malayalam literature, she gave a spirited reply that is worth citing at some length. What was true of Malayalam was also true of other literatures, but that is not because

women have no artistic talent, but because it is considered a great sin for women to speak their minds . . . [Society does not regard a woman as having] attained the stature of a person . . . society behaves as if, outside the home, a woman has no place between that of the ascetic (sanyasini) and the prostitute. Society should first accept a woman as a person. I know of many young women who have felt totally defeated because they were unable to satisfy their longing to write. No sooner does a woman write something than it starts a scandal. I often receive letters from girls who consider me a refuge. Even women whose writings have been accepted by society, who are well known and independent-minded, have had to endure a slur on their names. What would be the fate of the lesser known ones? How can women write when they are treated in this way? For a man, self-respect is a personal possession. A woman's reputation is a matter of life and death for the whole extended family. Under the circumstances no woman will be courageous enough to hurl herself into literature.[20]

What we know of the experiences of Lalithambika's contemporaries, K. Saraswathi Amma (1919–75) and Rajalekshmy (1930–1965), suggests that they might have agreed with her.[21]

Literary historians acknowledge that, "together with Kesava Dev, Thakazhi, and Ponkunnam Varkey, Lalithambika gave the Malayalam short story its strength and vigor. In the hands of these writers the short story became a weapon against the ills of society."[22] Yet she has received surprisingly little attention from the critical establishment.[23] Until very recently, scholars have restricted themselves to formalist assessments. They have praised the tight plots and the poetic language of a few stories, especially those of her middle period, singling out "The Devi and Her Devotee," "Life and Death" and "Admission of Guilt" for commendation. However, critics often complain that her writing is formally immature. "Goddess of Revenge," Sumangala writes, suffers from being too episodic and heterogeneous: description, comment, and autobiographical statement intrude on the fictional site.[24] It is evident from the memoir that her work was often dismissed as being too much concerned with reform, too little with aesthetics. More recently, mainly as a result of feminist initiatives, there has been a significant renewal of interest in her work.[25] I feel that even as I write in the late nineties, Lalithambika's own reflections and comments on her work still constitute its best criticism.

The stories and autobiographical essays chosen for translation here represent Lalithambika's major concerns: the plight of anterjanams who, more often than not, stand in for women as a whole; the nation's struggle for freedom; the dilemmas of a woman writer. Her concerns, which correspond to the inaugural concerns of our feminism, continue through the span of her writing, though her understanding and presentation change significantly. A reader might well trace through these texts a history of the women's movement, an ongoing feminist engagement with the aesthetic, a dream of the nation.

Madras 1997   GITA KRISHNANKUTTY

NOTES

1. Sreedhara Menon traces the beginnings of the spice trade back to the second millenium B.C. and the exchanges between Malabar and the Mesopotamian, Egyptian and Greek civilizations. See *A Survey of Kerala History* (Madras: S. Viswanathan, 1988), 45–53.
2. One theory of the Malayalam era, the Kollavarsham, is that it marks the extension of namboodiri authority to the southern town of Kollam and therefore to the whole of Kerala. See Menon, *A Survey*, 97–104.
3. Joseph Paimbilli, *Antherjanam: Oru Padanam* (Antherjanam: A Study) (Ramapuram: Antherjanam Sastiabdapurthi Celebration Committee, 1969, 107–108.
4. The poem has been translated as "Tragic Plight" by P.C. Gangadharan and published by the Kumaran Asan Memorial Committee, Thonnakal, Thiruvananthapuram district.
5. A long line of uprisings of Muslim peasantry against their Namboodiri landlords. Beginning in 1836, the rebellion continued into the twentieth century. Lalithambika writes principally about the 1920–1921 uprisings when the landlords were massacred. A reign of terror was unleashed by the British Government against the agitating Mapillas. These rebellions are also an important part of the early history of the Indian freedom struggle.
6. In 1921, B. Kalyani Amma had translated Tagore's novel directly from a serialized version called *At Home and Outside*, which had appeared in 1919 in *The Modern Review*, the influential literary journal in English that was edited by Ramananda Chattopadhyay (1865–1943) from Allahabad. The title, *Veetilum Purathum*, is the one Lalithambika would have been familiar with when she wrote her own novel.
7. Cited by K. Surendran, "Avatharika" (Introduction), *Therenjedutha Kathakal* (Kottayam: SPCS, 1966), 21.
8. See "A Writer Is Born" (*Ezhuthinte Eettillam*), this volume, p.144.
9. See, for example, *Malayala Manorama,* 26 July 1905 and 11 August 1905.
10. M. Leelavathi, *M. Leelavathi: Kavyarathi* (Thrissur: National Book Stall, 1993), 117.
11. See Dilip Menon, *Caste, Nationalism and Communism in South India: Malabar 1900–1948* (Delhi: Oxford University Press, 1994), 89–119; and Robin Jeffrey, *Politics, Women and Well-Being: How Kerala Became a "Model"* (Delhi: Oxford University Press, 1993), 118–126.
12. Akkamma Varkey, *1114nte Katha* (The Story of the Year 1114 [1938]) (Kottayam: D.C. Books, 1977). When told by an English soldier that he would have to shoot to disperse the crowd, Akkamma replied, "I am leading them now, shoot me first." Jeffrey, *Politics, Women and*

Well-Being, 124–125.

13. See Meena Alexander, "Outcaste Power: Ritual Displacement and Virile Maternity in Indian Women Writers," *Economic and Political Weekly* 24, 7 (1989): 367–372.

14. See "Childhood Memories" *(Balyasmriti),* this volume, p.133.

15. Leelavathi, *M. Leelavathi,* 121.

16. Jancy James, "Feminism as Social Commitment: The Case of Lalithambika Antherjanam," *Indian Literature* 173 (May–June 1996): 165.

17. Ibid, 170.

18. See "Lessons from Experience" *(Oru Kathikayude Anubhavapadangal),* this volume, p.157.

19. Foreword to *Atmakathakkoru Amukkham* (Thrissur: Current Books, 179).

20. Lalithambika Antherjanam, interviewed by T. N. Jayachandran, *Antherjanam: Oru Padanam,* 100.

21. See Susie Tharu and K. Lalita, eds., *Womens Writing in India,* vol. 2 (New York: The Feminist Press, 1993; Delhi: Oxford University Press, 1994), 164–170; 323–328; K. M. George, ed., *Inner Spaces: New Writing by Women from Kerala* (Delhi: Kali for Women, 1993).

22. M. R. Chandrashekharan in *Antherjanam: Oru Padanam,* 30.

23. The main critical work is a sixtieth birthday festschrift that includes several articles written especially for the occasion. Apart from that I have only been able to locate, with the help of Lalithambika's family, three essays in M. Leelavathi's 1993 book (n.10), part of a 1989 essay by the poet Meena Alexander (n.13), a 1990 essay mainly on "The Devi and Her Devotee" by N. Krishna Pillai and another essay by Jancy James (n.16).

24. *Antherjanam: Oru Padanam,* 64. See also N. Krishna Pillai, *Akaporul Thedi* (Thrissur: Sahitya Akademi, 1990).

25. See Susie Tharu and K. Lalita, eds. *Women Writing in India,* vols. 1 and 2 (New York: The Feminist Press, 1991, 1993; Delhi: Oxford University Press, 1992, 1994); and K.M. George, eds., *Inner Spaces.*

A NOTE ON THE TRANSLATION

In Malayalam, vocatives usually end with an "e." Thus the vocative of "Amma," is "Amme"; of "Ambika" is "Ambike" and of "Suma" is "Sume." This usage has been retained in the English translation. We have also attempted to preserve in our transliterations the Malayalam pronunciations of words, preferring therefore "anterjanam" to the Sanskritized "antharjanam" or "antherjanum" and so on. Non-English words are italicized the first time they appear in each piece. Every attempt has been made to gloss non-English words in the text itself provided they cannot be found in standard dictionaries like the *Oxford English Dictionary,* and the *Websters' Collegiate.*

Since Lalithambika consistently refers to the Kollavarsham or Malayalam era and not to the Gregorian calendar, we have also used those dates. The Kollavarsham begins in A.D. 825. We list below the months, with their English equivalents.

Chingam	August–September
Kanni	September–October
Thulam	October–November
Vrischikam	November–December
Dhanu	December–January
Makaram	January–February
Kumbham	February–March
Meenam	March–April
Medam	April–May
Edavam	May–June
Mithunam	June–July
Karkatakam	July–August

The kinship terms used are:

Amma	Mother
Achan	Father
Ettan	Elder brother
Chechi/Edathi	Elder sister
Muthassan	Grandfather
Muthassi	Grandmother

PART I

Stories

The Power of Fate

VIDHIBALAM

THE LITTLE HUT at the corner of the small compound was quite dilapidated. Through the dense smoke pouring out of its single door could be seen an emaciated young woman with disheveled hair, blowing at the fire. A six-year-old boy stood on the chipped platform outside the hut, nibbling at bits of tapioca that had been spread out to dry. A dog looked on eagerly, wagging its tail, and tossing its head to catch the morsels the boy threw indifferently in its direction from time to time.

Something stirred and moaned softly in the heap of smelly cloth piled up in a corner of the hut. The young woman, who had managed with great effort to light the fire, turned and asked, "What is it, Umma?"[1] Two hands as slender as matchsticks surfaced, and the heap of cloth moved to reveal a pitiful creature, all bones. A poet with a cruel sense of humor might have wondered why the woman found it so difficult to light a fire with such choice fuel in the room. But our own response is deep sympathy for this pathetic combination of poverty, disease, and utter helplessness.

"Come here, Pathumma," the woman called out in a feeble voice. The daughter went up to her. "The rice is just coming to the boil. Are you thirsty?"

"No, child. Sit down. I want to tell you something."

Pathumma sat down next to her. The old woman said, her voice full of tears, "I don't know if I'm right to ask you this, or if it will be possible. I want it so much. If I can't have it, child, I don't know why I should stay alive, a burden to the very earth."

Pathumma said tenderly, "Tell me, let me see if I can do it."

"You know the senior namboodiri of the *illam*? I want to see him before I die."

Pathumma was aghast. "The senior namboodiri! The head *thirumeni* of Vaishronath Illam! Do you really think he will visit our hut?"

"It is my greatest wish, child. Namboodiris always give in if you cry and plead with them. Yes, I know how hard-hearted they are and how cruelly they treat the poor. But you must go and try."

Pathumma was very upset. She was far more frightened of the namboodiri household than of the maharaja's palace. What would she say when she got there? Still, it was her mother's last wish.

"All right, I'll go. Shall I give you your *kanji* first?"

"The boy will give it to me. Go quickly, I want to know if he will come. I've waited so many years, hoping and longing for this."

Pathumma started out for the house, which was about ten miles away. She had been there once to buy paddy, and remembered the way vaguely. She stopped outside the huge wall. She knew that certain castes were not allowed beyond it, so she waited outside. There was so much noise, she thought it sounded like a fort in wartime. But she did not see a single living creature. When the day was well advanced, two nair women came out with vessels full of food, talking loudly.

"The feast was excellent, wasn't it, Amme? Amma Athol[2] must have given it her blessing."

Her mother responded sadly, "Blessing, indeed. Don't talk about her, I can't bear to think of her."

"Why, Amme, was she an evil person?"

"Evil? Siva! Siva! Far from it. She was the sweetest person I ever knew. But ruin was what she was fated for. She was four years younger than I. I wonder whether she's dead or alive now."

The daughter looked surprised. "How can they perform her *shraddha* if she's not dead?"

"It would have been better if she had died. They cast her out of the community. What a fate!"

"Why did they do that, Amme?"

"Do you think these namboodiris need a valid reason? I'm sure the young Athol was responsible for it. Once she arrived, the thirumeni began to detest the old Athol. They say it is she who instigated him to do what he did."

"Why did our young thirumeni allow it?"

"He was only ten years old at the time. Amma Athol wept uncontrollably when they cast her out. She screamed for her son. The little boy ran out to her, but the old thirumeni held him back and had him locked up. The child cried out, saying he wanted to go with his mother. I remember it all so well. The mapillas took that ravishingly beautiful woman away. I cried so much that day and beat my chest so hard that it still hurts."

"But how can they perform her shraddha, Amme, if she's still alive?"

"You don't understand, child. They shut the gates on her that day, cast her out, and performed the rites of the dead. They even observed the prescribed period of mourning. Who knows whether she's still alive, or whether she jumped into a river and drowned herself? It's possible that someone may have beaten her to death. Oh, God! It's better to be born a dog ten times over than to be born a woman in a namboodiri household!"

She caught sight of Pathumma and asked, "What are you doing here, you mapilla girl?"

Shocked by what she had just heard the women say, Pathumma managed to answer, "I came to request an audience with Thirumanassu."

"Are you mad, girl? Do you think Thirumanassu will deign to come out and see you? If you have something to say, talk to the *karyasthan*, Raman Nair."

"But it's something I have to say directly to Thirumanassu."

"You should have brought a gift, then. Anyway, you can't see him today. It is the day of his mother's shraddha. Even nairs will not be able to see him."

"When can I see him, then?"

"Ask Raman Nair. Come and see him tomorrow. And bring him a large quantity of yam or tapioca."

As Pathumma left, the old woman said to her daughter, "That mapilla girl has an amazing resemblance to Amma Athol. That's why I talked to her for so long."

When Pathumma got back, her mother was waiting impatiently for her.

"What happened, child?"

"I couldn't get to see him. They said it was his mother's shraddha today."

"His mother's shraddha! Narayana!" She quickly corrected herself, said, "Allah," and turned away. Some inner fire seemed to consume the withered frame.

The next morning, Pathumma gathered a handful of yams and a bunch of bananas and took them to the karyasthan's house. She waited in the courtyard till he came back from the illam. He looked at her gifts and seemed pleased with them.

"What do you want? Are you a tenant?"

"No. I have something to ask you."

"Tell me, whatever it is."

Pathumma said, very hesitantly, "I don't know whether you can do it for me—"

The karyasthan drew himself up arrogantly. "I can get anything I want done at the illam. But I have to approve of it first."

Pathumma spoke softly. "If the senior namboodiri would come to our hut. My old mother wants to see him before she dies."

Raman Nair became visibly agitated. "What an idea! Do you really expect him to come to your hut? He has hundreds of tenants. If they all made such extraordinary demands, what would he do?"

Pathumma began to cry. "Please don't say that. If the master wishes, he can do this for me. I'm sure of it. It is the old woman's last wish. God will surely bless the person who fulfills it."

The karyasthan looked offended. "Stop crying now and listen to me. Thirumeni will never pollute his feet by entering a mapilla hut. Tell me what you want and I'll try to get it done."

Pathumma suddenly had an idea. "God bless you, master. You

know Mammad—who has taken over the field next to us—well, he's begun to encroach on our compound. Thirumanassu can see for himself if he walks by our place, and the old woman will have her wish too. Master, we have no one except you to protect us. I'll come tomorrow with some more yams."

Raman Nair considered the proposition. Mammad was a scoundrel and had always been disrespectful to him. And Pachu Nair had offered him a bribe so that he could take over Mammad's field. Everything could be resolved in a single move. And this mapilla woman would have what she wanted as well. It wasn't such a bad idea.

"Come to the illam tomorrow afternoon, with a gift for the thirumeni. All you should say to him is that you would like him to come and see the field. You'll have trouble if you mention your mother. You had better cry and plead, he's sure to agree then."

Pathumma went away feeling happy. She prayed to Allah that her mother would live till the next day.

Vaishravanath Namboodiri usually had a bath early in the morning, performed his rituals and prayers, ate his morning meal, and came out to the veranda with his retinue by ten o'clock.

"Today's milk *payasam* was much better than yesterday's *prathaman*, wasn't it, Kareepram? It was delicious. I have a feeling that I took a little too much."

Taking no notice of the karyasthan, who stood waiting with a sheaf of papers, he disposed the weight of his ample stomach in a chair.

Kareepram, the practiced sycophant, removed the towel that lay over his shoulder and nodded his head.

"Yes, yes, today's payasam was excellent. Yesterday's prathaman was nothing compared to it."

Namboodiripad said, "I'll lie down for a while. Are the chessmen ready? Set them out, Kareepram."

The karyasthan saw that they were about to start a game. He cleared his throat hesitantly. Namboodiripad turned and looked at him.

"Ah, Raman, you've been waiting for quite some time, haven't you? Show me the papers I have to sign. Kareepram, take them from him."

The karyasthan handed over the sheaf of papers and waited respectfully, with his hand over his mouth. Namboodiripad glanced through the papers very casually, hardly reading any part of them, and got through the business of signing them. "Is that all for today?" he asked.

The karyasthan bowed deeply. "Yes, that's all there is to sign, but there are a couple of other matters. Mammad has become a menace to his neighbors. Pachu Nair says that if he can take over Mammad's field, he can give us a hundred *paras* more of paddy."

"No, no, that's not fair. Mammad is an old tenant and he never forgets to bring us gifts for Onam and Vishu."

"If Thirumanassu would come and see for himself, it would be a great help to the poor unfortunates. There's a mapilla girl waiting outside to explain how badly things are going for them."

"Deal with it yourself, Raman. Don't you know that's why I've appointed a karyasthan? I can't be bothered with these matters. Set out the pieces, Kareepram."

The karyasthan smiled meaningfully. "I think she's brought a gift."

Namboodiripad got up. "Well, we'll take a look at that. Come on, Kareepram."

Pathumma was waiting outside the huge stone walls. She bowed deeply before Namboodiripad and held out two clusters of creamy ripe poovan bananas on a plantain leaf. He smiled at her.

"What is your grievance, mapilla girl?"

She beat her chest and cried out loudly, "He's taken over our land and marked it into fields. Now he threatens to pull down our little hut."

"Who did this to you?"

"Mammad, the tenant. If Thirumanassu does not come and see for himself, and drive him away, all will be over with us."

"All right. I'll come tomorrow. Go home now."

Namboodiripad said on the way back, "Do you see now,

Kareepram, this is why I often think it's better not to have any property. All that it brings is misfortune."

Kareepram agreed. "Of course, of course."

The next evening, Namboodiripad and Kareepram went to inspect the field. The karyasthan followed them. Because he was very stout, Namboodiripad found it difficult to walk and also sweated profusely. But when he saw the rich grain ripening in his field, he was surprised and happy. "Look, Kareepram, it's the best land on the estate. Gems will sprout in such soil." He turned to Raman Nair. "It makes me furious when you tell me that we have debts."

"If you consider the expenditure—the household uses two thousand paras of paddy a month normally, and that is not counting the temple festivals, birthdays, and so on—"

"I've heard my father say that we have an income of nearly two lakhs."

Namboodiripad heard a pitiful groan from a hut near them.

"*Thampuran,* please come. You are our sole protector."

Namboodiripad looked distressed. His gentle heart was always susceptible to the sound of a sorrowful voice. Anyone who shed tears before him could get him to do anything.

"What is that, Raman? Is someone crying?"

"That's the hut of the mapilla girl we saw yesterday. I think that's where the sound came from."

"Thampuran, in the name of God, please come. Please don't delay," implored the voice again.

"Raman, go and find out what the matter is. Or wait, I'll come too. After all, if I'm polluted, I can go and have a bath."

Kareepram muttered, "If you enter a mapilla hut, we will have to perform all the purificatory rites." But Namboodiripad had walked on. A sense of status and a natural tenderness had fought for precedence in his heart, and tenderness had won.

Something that could barely be made out as a human form lay on the narrow platform of the hut on a tattered mat. Although death was struggling to claim the shriveled body, a sudden radiance surged through it when Namboodiripad entered. The old woman extended her wizened hands and beckoned to him. She could barely speak, "So this is how I see you again. What a fate!"

Namboodiripad stood very still, puzzled. He saw tears glistening in the eyes that were darkening with death.

"I've longed so much to see you. Come, Unni. All I want is for you to touch me once. I haven't touched you since you were ten." Namboodiripad suddenly recognized her. He did not know whether to remain there or to run away.

"They punished me for a sin I did not commit, my son. I've endured so much. Come, touch me once."

Namboodiripad thought confusedly of many things. However mistakenly she had been condemned, he felt that he could not touch a woman who had been cast out, who had lived with a *mleccha* for years and had two children by him. It would be a terrible sin! A namboodiri woman who had changed her religion was no better than a mleccha. It was a crime even to have looked at her! He did not say a word. He turned to go. But something suddenly moved him, and he stopped.

"I've seen her now and I'll have to do the purificatory rituals anyway. After all, she is my mother. Let me give her a few drops of water before she dies. Destiny brought me here. Raman, bring me some tulasi leaves."

Namboodiripad went up to her, chanting prayers. He put the tulasi leaves in water, recited the thousand names of Vishnu and poured the water, drop by drop, into her mouth. The mapilla hut echoed to the sound of Narayana's name. The old woman closed her eyes. She opened them a little later and saw Pathumma weeping. Her son was bewildered. She looked at Namboodiripad and said, "Unni, she's all alone in the world. The boy will earn a living somehow—"

Namboodiripad thought, how great is the dominance of desire even at the moment of death. He said, "Don't worry. God takes care of everyone."

"Not of me," she said. "If he did, I should have been right inside the *nalukettu* of the household now."

"But you're on my lap anyway. Look, how powerful fate is."

The old woman lapsed into silence. Her breath grew weaker.

Her soul soared in the joy of this unexpected good fortune. Namboodiripad continued to pour the tulasi water into her mouth.

"Allah! No, . . . Narayana!"

The body that had suffered infinite sorrow and pain dissolved into the essence of truth. Or at least that is what Namboodiripad, immersed in the intensity of prayer, believed.

Guiltily recalling his status, Namboodiripad got up. He looked at the frowning Kareepram and said, "Listen, Kareepram! Don't tell anyone about this. I couldn't help it, she's my mother after all. You can decide on whatever rituals of repentance I need to do. He turned to the karyasthan, "See that these people have whatever they need."

1932

NOTES

1. Mapilla word for mother.
2. Derived from *akathe aval* ("she who lives inside"). Added to the name of an anterjanam.

In the Moonlight

NILAVELICCHATHIL   2

ANNAMME, DID I hear you whispering? I won't have that, understand? I won't have you flirting with my son even before you've crossed the threshold of our house."

Annamma's mother-in-law peered out of the narrow, smoke-encrusted kitchen door, shaking her head hard in such disapproval that the long *kunukkus* in her ears rocked ominously. "It's dreadful. Young people are so shameless these days."

Anna called back from the courtyard where she sat oiling a pot, "I wasn't talking to anyone. I was just shooing away the crow that had overturned the pot."

"Now that's a lie if I ever heard one. I know Avuda is somewhere there. I saw him walk that way a minute ago. Avude!" she called out authoritatively. "What were you doing, working near the girl?"

"Nothing. I just happened to be walking by."

"There you are, I knew the girl was lying. Shooing away crows, indeed! I know what you're up to, my girl. Don't imagine that a chit like you can throw dust in my eyes! Listen to me, young fellow, what I have to say is meant for you too. If this sort of thing happens just once more, you'll have cause to remember!"

Avuda strode away without a word. There was so much he had to do, anyway. Anna turned and walked slowly to the well, crying, her eyes reddened. Lost in her thoughts, she threw in the palm spathe and swirled it as she bent over to draw the water. She had no eyes for the green spreading over the walls of the well, or for the water moving in its depths, although its eddying surface mirrored her own agitated heart.

They had been married almost six months now. Avuda was sixteen, Anna fifteen, but she was a whole foot taller than him. Young girls grow rapidly, and tire of growing just as fast.

Theirs was a household that adhered very rigidly to the Catholic custom of not allowing newlyweds to meet or to talk to each other. And Anna's mother-in-law seemed exceptionally clever at ensuring that this custom was strictly observed. Recalling the ruses she had resorted to herself when as a new bride she had wanted to meet her husband in secret, she exercised great vigilance to stop the young people from doing the same things. Of course, where Avuda was concerned, all this was totally unnecessary. He was still a boy, immersed in his activities, as yet untouched by the heady stirrings of passion. Soon after their marriage, he had spoken to Anna a few times, in the innocent companionship of youth. But he no longer did so because he was afraid of his mother.

Anna, however, was not quite as guiltless as he was. She longed to talk to Avuda and sought out occasions to do so. She would steal up to him while he was at work in the field, and, if there was no one around, she would jab provocatively at his smooth hairless cheek with her finger. Avuda never quite knew what it all meant, but Anna was perfectly aware of what she was doing.

"Why are you poking my cheek?" he would turn and ask innocently. "Is it a jackfruit or a mango that you must prod to find out whether it is ripe?"

"Oh, I just did it for fun," she would reply, turning her eyes down, and smiling as she walked off.

Having worked very hard all day, digging and turning the earth, Avuda would come back at dusk, devour whatever his mother served him, curl up on his mat, and begin to snore. And what of Anna, in her corner of the kitchen? She would lie awake, tossing and turning, watching the slivers of moonlight that broke through the crevices in the wall.

Thus the days went by. Soon, it was Christmas. It was the grandest festival of the year in their church. Both her parents-in-law were going to church. Someone had to stay home to look after the house and the many farm tools lying around in the yard. The older pair ate their dinner early, locked Anna in the house, and set out for the service at midnight.

"Avude, go to the watchman's shed and sleep there. Make sure nothing gets stolen."

All dressed up in her forty-year-old finery, the old woman walked to church. Anna could not sleep. She was still awake at midnight, pacing the little room like a caged animal. She tried each one of the locked doors, but they were too strong for her to break open. Was there no other way? She looked up, and a sudden thought struck her. Beneath the rafters, extending into the low wall, was a small crevice. She lifted herself up to it, wiggled her way through like a bandicoot, and leaped out. Her back and her elbows were grazed, but what did that matter? She stole round to the watchman's shed. There was Avuda, curled up on a torn mat near the fire pit, snoring. She stroked his back gently and said, "Imagine being so fast asleep. If a thief were to come, you'd never know."

He started awake and looked up at her.

"Who is it—you? How did you sneak out? What a fright you gave me!"

"I was scared, lying there, all alone. So I crept out through a gap in the wall," she said. "The moon is so bright tonight. Why should I lie there, suffocating, inside the house?"

"Go back and lie down. If Appan[1] and Amma come back now, they'll kill me." Avuda was truly terrified.

"They won't be back so soon," she consoled him. "Can't you hear, the band has just begun to play?"

"If Amma feels sleepy, they'll start back early. Don't drag me into this. Just go away."

"They've gone together, haven't they? Can't the two of us be together too? Why did they get us married if we can't even talk to each other?"

She smiled meaningfully at him.

"You can talk all you want. It's me they'll beat up when Amma gets back. Go back in and lie down. Don't bother me like this."

It was a rough response and it hurt the young girl deeply. As she walked back disconsolately in the moonlight, her face grew serious with the weight of a grave decision. Avuda knew nothing of this. Indifferent as always, he had lain down on his torn mat and fallen sound asleep.

When the mother-in-law returned early the next morning, Anna was nowhere to be found. All the locks were in place.

"What can it mean? Where is she? Could she have been spirited away by some demon? Avude, did you see her last night?"

"How could I have seen her? I was outside." He drew himself up to his full length to emphasize his innocence.

"Amazing. How did she manage to get out of a locked room?"

They searched everywhere for Anna, and found her at last in her father's house, seventeen miles away. She had arrived there at daybreak.

"We don't want such a willful, undisciplined girl in our family. Avuda will not miss her," her father-in-law shouted as he turned back, furious.

Two years passed. Avuda was no longer the same person. He had grown taller and stronger. Weeds began to take root in his mind, like the black stubble sprouting on his chin. For some inexplicable reason, he had begun to think more and more of Anna. Suddenly, it seemed, he was impatient to see her again. She must have grown. What a beautiful woman she must be now. What if he went to see her?

He said to his mother one day, as she worked hard in the kitchen, "Why don't we get her back, Amme? Things would be easier for you."

"No, no, I don't want her, or any other girl. As long as I'm alive, you'll not bring back a girl who left all by herself, and that too, at the dead of night. I can see what you're after, you rascal."

He did not pursue the matter and his mother continued to slave over the housework.

Christmas came round again. Avuda lay alone in the watchman's shed. The tapioca and climbing yams lay bathed in the pearly white moonlight. The scent of mango blossoms wafted on the soft breeze. A koel perched on a mango branch sang "kuhu-kuhu" to its mate. The happy sounds of Thiruvathira[2] dancing flowed out of the neighboring houses. The very air seemed intoxicated, as if nature itself thrilled to the coming of the loveliest season, spring.

Avuda rose. There was a deep ache in him, as though he had lost something. What was it? His mind turned to that night two years ago. He remembered how she had come to him, and how hard it had been for her to do so. And he had simply turned her away! He was just beginning to understand. He stood in the yard uneasily, wondering what to do. It was midnight. The moon was high in the sky, but a veil of mist blurred its radiance.

Coward that he was, he first armed himself with a stick. Then he walked on fearlessly. He arrived at Anna's house at daybreak, at the very same hour that she had got there, two years ago. Her parents were taken aback. Clearly, he had not had a thought for her all this time, yet here he was, on the doorstep, impatient to see her. How strange it was. They concealed their surprise, however.

Throughout the next day, he waited for an opportunity to be alone with Anna but managed it only by dusk, when he found her watering the vegetables. She bent her head when she saw him and hid her face behind the water pot. A reproachful sigh escaped her.

"Anna, have you forgotten me?" he asked sadly. "I made a terrible mistake. I was such a child then, and so ignorant. We must never part again. I'm going to build my own house!" He confessed his guilt and comforted her, all in the same breath. Anna's eyes filled. This happiness was so unexpected. "Are you crying? What did I say, to make you cry? Don't, please don't. I can't bear it."

A snake gourd that she had just watered raised its head, moist and fresh, the glare of the afternoon sun forgotten. It put out a new tendril that curled tenderly on to the bower above.

1937

NOTES

1. Syrian Christians of Kerala call their father Appan or Appachan, their mother Amma or Ammachy.
2. A festival in December that women celebrate by singing and dancing in groups.

The Goddess of Revenge

PRATICARADEVATHA   3

IT WAS NEARLY midnight. I was sitting alone in the room where I usually did all my writing. The compassionate Goddess of Sleep stood by me, waiting to enfold in her caress the wounds that my spirit had accumulated in the course of the day's hard work. But I knew that if I threw down the pen and paper I had taken up to write my story, I would not be able to touch them again till the same time tomorrow, when the usual obstacles would again present themselves. I sat there wrapped in thought. Silence lay deep around me, interrupted now and then by the sounds of two rats engaged in love talk in the attic above, or the snores of the children sleeping in the next room. The light from the lamp on the table crept out through the window and cast fearful shadows onto the thick darkness outside. The hooting of the many owl families that were my neighbors sounded like a warning in my ears. I must confess: I am a coward by nature. Especially at this deceptive hour of the night.

I closed and bolted the window and raised the wick of the lamp. I checked whether any of the children were awake or whimpering, then came back to my usual place. I had to finish writing today, come what may, but what was I going to write about? How was I to begin? Now that I had sat down to write, all the attendant problems rose up to confront me. Writing stories is not a pleasant task, especially for a woman like me, for whom status and prestige and a sense of being highborn are all-important. When fictional characters come to life and argue heatedly about contemporary issues, the author has to face opposition from many quarters. If an opponent were to use the weapon of obscene language against me, would I be able to defend myself with a like weapon? And then, the subject of caste distinctions was taboo, and religious controversies were to be avoided at all costs. Indeed, we have arrived at a point when writers have perforce to consider well in advance which particular literary theorist's recriminations they would have to face. It was all very distressing. I suddenly wanted to give it all up.

Filled with an obscure sense of anger, I threw my pen onto the table, and closed my eyes. Innumerable characters passed through my mind as I sat there: people I had seen and not seen, people who were alive and who were dead. Women and men. Creatures tormented by pain, those who had lost their voices, though their throbbing hearts thudded like thunderclouds, flashed like lightning. Were they demanding to be transcribed? I was afraid, but also inspired. Suddenly, I heard the sound of footsteps coming toward me from the next room.

What could it mean? I sat up, startled. I had closed the door, bolted it securely, and locked it. And I had not even heard it being pushed open. It was midnight. Although I did not believe in ghosts, I trembled in fear. My head began to spin. My eyes closed tight. The footsteps grew firmer and firmer. Someone came and actually stood next to me, but I could not move.

The seconds ticked by. Did five minutes pass, or a whole hour? I couldn't say. Time stopped for a long while. Then I heard a woman's voice, just in front of me, a firm yet fine and delicately modulated voice. "Are you asleep? Or afraid?" she asked.

I remained very still. I did not have the strength to move, anyway. The voice went on, its sweetness tinged with a shade of mockery, "When I heard that you wrote stories, I did not imagine that you would be such a coward. After all, a good writer usually has to witness so many scenes of agony and terror."

The eagerness to know the identity of this person, who knew so much about me, drove my fear away. I opened my eyes. In front of me, the figure of a woman took shape from the surrounding texture of a dream. A woman . . . not a young girl. Not bold or proud. Not old either. All I can say is that she seemed a wonderful manifestation of meaning itself. Sorrow, a certain austerity, disgust, disappointment: all struggled to find expression in her face. The sparks of an intense fire burned fearfully in her eyes—I recognized the emotion as from the leaves of some forgotten book from the distant past. She went on in a voice powerful yet tender.

"I've come with a purpose. I know you are looking for a story to write, but are unable to find one. I have a first-class story, which is going to waste for want of someone to use it. If you agree . . . if you can listen to it without being terrified . . . "

I had mustered my courage by now. "It's true that I panicked. But that's because of the time and the circumstances. Please, for heaven's sake, tell me who you are, and how you got here at this time of the night through a locked door."

"Who am I?" She burst out laughing. "So you want to know who I am, do you? Whether I'm a human being, or an evil spirit, a ghost, or a witch. What superb courage!"

She laughed out loud again, sounding like a forest stream that breaks its banks and overflows. Her laughter thudded against the walls of the room. But this time I did not wince.

"I confess that I am a coward," I said. "But how can I have anything to do with you unless I know who you are? Human beings come to know the very stars in the sky by giving them names and positions of their own."

"Human beings? For heaven's sake, don't count me among them, Sister," she interrupted, looking displeased. "There was a time when I loved to be known as a human being, when I expended my greatest efforts on staying as one. But I have learned—and taught others—that I never want to be called a human being again, and particularly not a woman. To be human, how deceitful it is, how cruel, what an experience of agony."

"Maybe you are right," I admitted. "But pain and agony are gifts that are granted only to human beings. They are links in a divine chain of gold."

She shook her head and prevented me from going on. "Stop this foolish raving: 'divine,' 'gold.' What melodious descriptions! A 'chain of gold' indeed. Let me ask you, what advantage do golden chains have over iron ones if they are meant to be fetters? Only this: that iron shows its true colors. And gold? What a glitter. A mere coating. God! What does it prove but the difference between a human being and a demon?"

Her face, which was full of hatred for her fellow beings, seemed transformed into something nonhuman. I could not be certain whether her expression signified sorrow, hatred, pride, or revenge, but I found it a singularly attractive mixture of all these emotions, and my eyes were riveted on her. What deep despair, what grief this life must have borne!

"So you're waiting to hear my story," she continued, after a short silence. "All right, I've come for that anyway. It is an old story. It happened more than fifty years ago, and it is a true story, one that shook the world to its foundations when it happened. You had not been born then, neither had your social organizations, with their penchant for debate, nor their leaders. And yet the turmoil that this story created over a great part of Kerala still continues. Some of the characters who figured in it may still be alive. Have you heard of Tatri?"

Oh, oh, so this was she. I drew back sharply in fear. This was the woman whose name our mothers had forbidden us even to utter, the very memory of whose name awakened horror. This was—oh, what could I say?

She smiled with evident delight at my distress. "Yes, yes, you're thinking, which namboodiri woman has not heard of that unfortunate creature, aren't you? No one says so in so many words. But everyone knows. But, look, child! Do you know for whom, for what that ill-fated sadhanam[1] sacrificed her life? She too was a pure and untainted young woman once, like all of you. She wove chains of sacred karuka grass. She recited her prayers with a holy thread in her hands. She performed all the ritual fasts. She was as meek as a doll; after the age of ten she never looked at a man's face, or spoke to him. Grandmothers advised young girls who had reached puberty to learn from Tatri's shining example. But you and I know that all this is part of an outward show. By the time we are seventeen or eighteen, we acquire an amazing capacity to keep our feelings under control. As we sit in the veranda by the light of the new moon, chanting our prayers, we hold the sighs that rise in our hearts in ourselves; no one ever hears them. Singing the "Parvathi Swayamvaram," the "Mangalayathira,"[2] and other auspicious marriage songs, moving our feet in time to their rhythm, we learn to control the trembling in our throats. Yet, do we not listen to the sound of men's footsteps from the living room? Even while struggling with the prickly exasperating kuvalam flowers, our hearts are full of the fragrance of mango blossoms. And we wait. Not just days and months, but years. Till at last one day our mothers come to us with henna and a silver ring. Whether our hands are placed in those of an old man or a young one, a sick man or a libertine is all a matter of destiny. We can do nothing but endure.

"People told me that I had been singled out for a very special destiny. I was his first wife. And he was not an old man either. He had enough to live on at home. So I started married life with a boundless sense of happiness. He was a passionate man. I nurtured my desires to suit his. I did my utmost to satisfy him in bed, with the same attention with which I prepared food to please his palate. After all, a husband is considered to be a god. It was to give pleasure to this god that I learned a harlot's ways, those talents that were to become so notorious later. It was he who taught them to me. If it had been otherwise, my sister! If I too had become a meek wife, ignored by her husband, like countless women in our society, I wonder whether this cursed happening would have been blown so much out of proportion. I don't know. Maybe the intoxication of physical pleasure crept insidiously into my mind and lingered there as a fragrance. But he was the only person enclosed within that fragrance, I swear it. That is why I was so upset when we began to drift apart gradually. He began to stay away from home for many nights in succession. Occasionally, it was to perform a religious rite, or to attend a temple festival. He would stay in rich princely homes then. When we met, more and more rarely, I would weep before him, find fault with him. To whom could I unburden my sorrows, except to him?

"He would laugh, indifferent to the pleas of a broken heart. Man is free. He lives for pleasure. Just because he was married—and to an uninteresting namboodiri woman—it did not mean that he had to waste his youth on her.

"Anger and fury sharpened within me. I wanted to batter myself, I wanted to die. I even cursed myself for having been born. Why had I been born a namboodiri woman? Couldn't I have been born into some other caste in Kerala, some caste that would have given me the right to pay this arrogant man back in his own coin?

"And yet, on his every birthday, I bathed and prayed for a long and happy married life. I offered ghee lamps and garlands of thumba flowers in the temple. All I wanted now was to see him sometimes so that I could fill my eyes with his presence. Just as when I had reached puberty I had begun to pray for a husband, I longed now for my husband's love.

"Thanks to the generosity of our *karyasthan* we did not starve. But emotions and sensations have their own hunger, don't they? Greed. Thirst. Once brought to life, they cannot be quelled. They creep into the bloodstream, into the veins, they melt in them and simmer there. That was what happened to him too. But then, he was a man and I a woman, a woman born into a cursed society.

"Like all *anterjanams*, I too endured, kept my feelings in check, and carried on. It happened, without any warning: one evening, he came home with his new wife. They slept in the very room where I had slept with him. I did not mind serving food to that harlot. But though I had read Shilavathi's[3] story a hundred times, making their bed was—Although I was a namboodiri woman, I was a human being too. Maybe I had accused her of being a prostitute. Maybe I had cursed her for being a slut and a harlot. This was the first time I thought of men as monsters, the first time my husband became a murderer in my eyes. I could have borne the torture for myself. But when he, my husband, used the same words—'I brought her home deliberately, knowing she's a harlot. I like harlots. Why don't you become one yourself?'—what a cruel blow that was.

"Even to think of it petrifies me. Imagine a husband telling his chaste, highborn wife, a woman who worships him, 'If you want me to love you, you must become a prostitute.' An irrational, uncontrollable desire for revenge took hold of me. But only for an instant. My faith stood in the way. 'No, I can't remain here, even for a single day.'

"After that I never spoke to him again. I never spoke to anyone. The days went by somehow, empty of events, empty of love. If only something would move in this hell of darkness! I went back to the house where I was born, my heart full of limitless grief, a burden of sorrow that it could hardly bear. I thought I would find comfort and relief at home, but I was wrong. In truth, are not all namboodiri households a kind of prison? There is little to choose between them. My father was dead, but all his five wives were still alive. My elder brother was looking for a wife to replace his fourth one who had just died. Two of my older sisters, both widowed, were living at home. The third one had gone mad because her namboodiri husband had tortured her, and she wandered about here and there. Two unmarried younger sisters had become a burden on the house, a continual source of worry to their mother. I joined them, going from the frying pan into the fire. Amid such grief, who would not long for whatever comfort society permitted? I was still young. My body bloomed with health. I knew I could afford the arrogance of being certain that I was more beautiful than the prostitutes who kept my husband company. And yet, when I combed my hair, placed the bright red *sinduram* between my eyebrows, and peered out through the barred door, all I felt was a desire to see the world, or, at most, an innocent longing that someone should notice how beautiful I was. There were men who met my eyes, returned my smile. After all, people tend to smile if you smile at them. It soon became a habit. Were not those highborn brahmins susceptible precisely because they knew I was a namboodiri woman? They were aware of the consequences. But as long as nobody was aware of what they did, they indulged in the basest actions.

"Scandalous reports began to spread. And meaningful looks. I heard murmurs. The women's quarters turned into a fifth column. Amma cursed whenever she caught sight of me. 'You sinner, born to ruin the family's honor! Why were you ever born in my womb?'

"My brother's wife said one day, 'Tatri, don't come into the kitchen anymore. I'd rather you didn't touch anything there.'

"I did not understand the nature of the crime for which I was being punished. I had touched no man except my husband. I had not even dared to think of another man that way. If I peered out of the window, if someone saw me and was attracted to me, how could that be my fault? But the world does not concern itself with such questions. My heart hardened as stones of mockery were hurled at me. My mind whirled with the fear of disgrace. Then suddenly I knew that I could take anything that came to me. I had reached a point where I could bear anything. Darkness surrounded me on all sides. My enemies hissed at me like poisonous serpents in a smoke-filled darkness. They stung me, bit me. To defend myself in this battle unto death, I had to become a poisonous serpent too. The desire for revenge and the hatred that had lain dormant within me blazed high. If I tell you about the decision they forced me to, you will draw back in fear. You will tremble and drive me out of here. Oh, my sister, what I did was as much for your sake as for mine. For the sake of all namboodiri women who endure agonies. So that the world would realize that we too have our pride. I wanted to prove that we have strength and desire and life in us too. I delighted in the sorrow each man had to bear, for not a single tear shed by a namboodiri woman has value. But alas, all of you, for whom I did this, despised me. My very name was uttered with disgust in my lifetime. I was feared more than a demon. Even in the fashionable world of today, Tatri remains despicable; even you look upon me as a fallen and disgraced woman."

Her voice trembled at this point. Her eyes filled. Weighed down by an unbearable sadness, she put her head down on the table. Silently, without moving, I watched that personification of hopelessness. The destiny of a woman like her, placed in such a situation, could take so many directions. If that broken life were to disintegrate completely, if its shattered remnants were to be scattered on the roadside like fragments of broken glass, surely it could not be her fault. Only the base tenets that had made her what she was could be blamed. For a namboodiri woman who feels the heat of emotion, who feels proud to be alive, there is only one of two ways possible: she must go mad, or fall from grace. Both ways are hard.

Maybe she had no tears left to shed. She sat up. A flame that would have burned up even the fires of hell blazed in her eyes.

"No, child! I will not cry anymore. This is my last moment of weakness. I knew I would never be terrified again, not even if the seas swept over me or the skies fell down. Fear ceases to exist when life and death seem no different from each other. I had made my decision. If this was to be my ultimate destiny, I would trans-form it into an act of revenge. I would avenge my mothers, my sisters, countless women who had been weak and helpless. I laid my life, my soul, everything I possessed, at this sacrificial altar of revenge and sought the blessings of the gods. Let everyone see— and learn—that not only man but also woman could bring herself down to the lowest level. My capacity to err would have to be strong enough: if I were to be cast out of society, if I were to be ostracized, I wanted to make sure that I was not innocent. No one was going to punish me for a crime that I had not committed. If I were going to be pushed aside, others who were mean and cruel were going to fall with me. I wanted people to learn a lesson. If there was true justice, would it not be necessary to cast out more namboodiri men than women?

"From that night onward, a new face was seen at all the temple festivals, the face of a fascinating courtesan. She was passionate and beautiful. But more than her loveliness, it was a bewitching air of shyness, a gentleness of nature, that attracted men to her. Princes, titled chiefs, and many other well-known men crowded around her. I told them all that I was a married woman and not a prostitute. I told them I had a husband, I told them everything, offering them a chance to break free. The only thing I hid from them was that I was a namboodiri woman. But the answer that they gave never varied: that bondage to a husband was not stipu-lated in this land of Parasurama,[4] and that all women, except the namboodiris, were free here. They could do what they liked. This was the pattern of their comforting excuses. Oh, the minds of these men, who pretended to be self-respecting, pure, and saintly, even ascetic. If only men who insisted that their wives remain chaste did not deliberately seduce other men's wives.

"Would not a woman who was aware that so many were attracted to her succumb, finally, in spite of herself? Particularly one con-demned to the inner rooms of a namboodiri household, whom other women spat on and kicked? It was an age when the greed for flesh knew no bounds. The fame of this new harlot spread far and wide. Those who came to her went away gladdened. And she did not forget to persuade them to express their satisfaction through gifts. Thus the reputation of many who swaggered as honorable men of society came into the keeping of this prostitute.

"Only one man was left to come to me. The man I had waited for unceasingly. Surely, he would not fail to come when he heard of this beautiful strong-willed woman, for he loved passionate encounters. It was five years since we had met. Although I recognized him when we met at the trysting place in the temple courtyard, he did not make me out. How could he have? How could anyone have guessed that this proud and confident woman, this jewel among prostitutes, was that humble namboodiri wife of long ago?

"That was an unforgettable night. It was the night I had lived for, for so long, the night for which I had let myself be degraded. At least I was able to delight him for once. Ever since he had said to me, 'Go and learn to be a prostitute,' his command had lain simmering in my consciousness. If a woman who learns the ways of a prostitute in order to delight her husband can be considered chaste, I was another Shilavathi. I think it was a blissful night for him too. For, a little while before we parted, he said to me, 'I have never been with anyone as intelligent and as beautiful as you. I wish I could always stay with you.'

"He had trapped himself. As he slipped his ring on my finger, I asked, 'Are you certain that you've never met anyone like me?'

"He lifted his sacred thread, held it high in his hand, and swore, 'By this wealth I possess as a brahmin, this symbol of my caste, I have never seen a woman as passionate and as intelligent as you in all my life.'

"A triumphant smile was on my lips. I raised my voice a little and said, 'That's a lie. Remember your wife. Was she not as pleasing as I am?'

"Light dawned on him. Suddenly, he looked at my face and screamed, 'Ayyo, my *Vadakkunnathan*! It is Tatri! Tatri! Tatri!' Then he fled, I do not know where he went or when he stopped.

"The story is nearly over. You know what happened after that.

The affair provoked a smartavicharam[5] that rocked Kerala to its very foundations. From great prince to highborn brahmin, men trembled, terrified because they did not know whose names this harlot was going to betray. Some men ran away and escaped. Others performed propitiatory rites, praying that she would forget their names during the cross-examination.

"One man's ring with his name engraved on it. Another's gold waist chain. Yet another's gold-bordered *angavastram*. The incriminating pieces of evidence were used to prove the guilt of sixty-five men, including *vaidikans*. I could have caused not just these sixty-five but sixty thousand men to be cast out of the community. And not I alone. In those days, any lovely and intelligent woman who practiced this profession could have brought ruin upon entire families of landlords and wealthy aristocrats. And yet I did not go that far, even though I knew the power of a namboodiri woman's curse. That historic trial had to end there. A longstanding grievance was assuaged. Was it simply an act of revenge performed by a prostitute? Or was it also the expression of the desire for revenge experienced by all namboodiri women who are caught in the meshes of evil customs, who are tortured and made to suffer agonies? Tell me, Sister! Who is more culpable, the man who seduces a woman in order to satisfy his lust, or the woman who transgresses the dictates of society in an attempt to oppose him? Whom would you hate more? Whom would you cast out? Give me an answer at least now, after so many years have gone by."

I had sat dazed, unable to utter a single word, while she recounted this extraordinary story. I was frozen, helpless.

Remarking on my silence, she continued with an air of profound hopelessness, "Perhaps I've made a mistake. Why did I come here today? Why did I try to talk to yet another of those anterjanams who are without shame or self-respect, another slave among slaves? They will never learn to improve their lot. Never." Her voice trembled with anger and grief.

But I felt no anger toward her. I said to her softly, "My poor sister! I am not trying to find fault with you. On the contrary, I have deep sympathy for you. Truly, you are not an individual anymore; you are society itself. You are timidity and weakness weeping before strength, helpless womanhood screaming for justice, bloodstained humanity whose desires and talents have been ground into dust.

"How can the expression of irremediable hopelessness and help-lessness be identified with your own? Consider, there is another side to all this. I have been thinking about it. Fired as you were with the intoxication of revenge, why did you not try to inspire all the other weak and slavish anterjanams? Why did you shoulder the burden of revenge all alone? In such matters, Sister, individuals cannot triumph. On the other hand, they can bring disaster upon themselves. Consider, now, what good did that hurricane you set in motion do to society? Men began to torture anterjanams all the more, using that incident as a weapon. We are close now to bowing our heads once again under the same yoke. Not even the women in the families of the sixty-five who were cast out have been re-leased from their agony."

I too was shaken. I continued, my voice trembling, "So, forgive me, Tatri sacrificed her very soul, but in the eyes of the world her sacrifice is remembered only as a legal affair involving a prosti-tute—an affair that certainly created a turmoil, but did not succeed in pointing the way to anything positive. The end cannot justify the means, Sister. Even while I recognize your courage and self-re-spect, I disagree with you. But namboodiri society can never forget Tatri. From the heart of a great silence, you managed to throw out an explosive, a brightly burning spark. It was a brave warning, a cry of victory. In the minds of the generations to come, this cry ignited a torch that still burns high and threatening. In its radiance, all the sins of that praticaradevatha, that Goddess of Revenge, are forgiven."

I held out my hands to that woman's form in affection and sym-pathy. Its face paled. Its eyes grew lifeless. "Oh, I am a sinner. A fallen woman. An evil spirit. Even my shadow must never fall over society."

Continuing to talk, her form faded slowly, dissolving like the morning mist. The crowing of the cock woke me from my dream.

1938

NOTES

1. See Introduction, p.xxii.
2. Traditional songs that women sing and dance to, in seeking the blessings of Siva and Parvathi for long and happy married lives.
3. The archetypal figure of a selfless woman whose life is given to pleasing her husband.
4. See Introduction, p.xiv.
5. Trial. See Introduction, p.xxii.

Admission of Guilt

KUTTASSAMMATHAM 4

THE THING, SADHANAM, who had been kept in isolation and charged with adultery was summoned to the court convened by the elders of her community.[1] She said in her statement: "I am guilty. Cast me out if you will. But I, and only I, am entirely responsible for all that has happened. No other person shares my guilt."

A stir rose in the assembly. What effrontery! A pregnant widow insisting that no one else had a part in her sin! How then had she committed it?

The *smartan* roared, "Whore! We know you have transgressed. Why can't you tell us the truth now?"

A voice choked with sobs flowed out of the *anchampura.*

"As God is my witness, I tell you that I do not know who is to blame. Was it the loneliness of that night? Or my youth? Or the persuasive power of certain sensations I had never known or experienced till then? You all know that I was a child widow. They broke the thread that held my *thali* when I was fourteen. That was twenty years ago. There has been no taint on my reputation till now. I never once broke my Monday fasts. I observed the ritual baths prescribed in the month of Magha, rites sacred to the month of Vaisakha,[2] without fail. I never missed the monthly worship at the Thripprangot and Guruvayur temples. Why then did God put this evil thought into my head just that one night? I have spoken to no man save my father. The very thought of men terrified me. For there is only one man that a woman should know, and for me he does not exist.

"My world was limited to the kitchen and the *vadikkini*. Never once did I open the door of the *nalukettu,* even to look out. And yet, this happened to me. Why did it happen? I'll tell you the story. Whether you believe me or not, it's the truth."

It was an astonishing opening statement. The court was paralysed. How could this fallen woman justify her behavior when the accusation against her was so clear? The *vaidikan* grunted a reluctant consent: "Let what is to be said be said quickly."

The door opened a little and a stream of sound flowed like an unrestrained waterfall through the narrow crevice into the outside world.

"I know you will consider it a sin to hear my story, a sin even to hear my voice. I too thought as you did once—that an *anterjanam* who has been cast out was more contemptible, more vile, than a demon. I was careful to see that no such stories, not even a whiff of air from where they arose, ever touched me. Even when Tatri Edathi was on her deathbed, I refused to visit her. Perhaps it was for that terrible crime that, now—

"I don't need to go back to the beginning. You were all there at the wedding feast that day, a part of the crowd. What was it about that hour that you found so auspicious? The thirty-year-old daughter of a senior namboodiri who was to be my husband came into our family, and I was given in exchange. I was eleven years and three months old at the time. The two fathers married each other's daughters, a good exchange. Muthassi used to say, 'At least we were able to give the child away before she reached puberty, although I do not know how she will cope with those terrible people.'

"I didn't have to cope with them for long. For my father's bride, my new mother, was a sick woman. She died very soon. I became a burden to the old man who was my husband. You know that when such things happen, women usually go back to their fathers' households. My mother was still my father's favorite wife, so I was happy at home.

"I have looked at my husband's face only once. He had a gray beard and a mustache and a potbelly. I felt more bewildered than frightened when I saw him. Muthassi tried her best to persuade me to go to his room, but I would not go. And so that man, who had married four namboodiri wives and lived with forty nair women,[3] never returned to our house. It could have been his curse, for only two more years went by—

"One evening, during the Onam season, I was in the outer court-yard playing ball with my friends, when I heard a servant enter from the other side of the house. My father whispered something to my mother.

"'Ayyo! My child—oh, God, you've betrayed me!'

"My mother beat her chest with her hands and fell to the ground. Everyone gathered around her. There was a small commotion. I was snatched away from where I was playing contentedly with my friends, and dragged indoors. There was loud wailing in the kitchen. Even so, I did not cry. I could think of no reason to cry.

"I bathed in the tank, came in streaming wet, and lay down in a dark room. I took off my bell metal bangles. I wiped the *thilakam* off my forehead. I did everything they asked me to do. But when, according to custom, the senior daughter-in-law of the household came to break the sacred black thread I wore around my neck, I protested. 'l won't give it to you. I won't take off my thali. Ask Amma, I hold that thread in my hands every day while I chant the thousand and eight holy names.'[4]

"My obstinate protest reached my father's ears. He came to the door of my room, his grief showing very clearly on a face ravaged by old age. 'Give it to her, child. Father will get his daughter a really lovely chain, much better than this one, in ten days' time.'

"I knew my father would keep his word. When the funeral rites were over, I was given a tulasi patterned chain made of gold in place of the broken thali. How brightly it glowed! How beautiful it was! My whim was satisfied. If only I had remained as ignorant now, as I was then, of the difference between that thali and this chain—

"I slowly got used to the changes I had to make in my daily routine. No longer might I touch the *ashtamangalyam* or the lamp. No longer might I put kohl in my eyes, or a thilakam on my forehead. I might eat rice only once a day. It was Muthassi who taught me how I should dress, how to carry myself, how to behave. I would lie on her lap and listen to her tell old stories. That was how I first learnt the stories of Sri Krishna, of the *gopikas* and of Brindavanam.

"When each story was over, Muthassi would say, her expression gently sorrowful, 'Bhagavan! Guruvayurappan! You must chant Krishna's name. That is your life's work now.'

"I asked, 'Where is Bhagavan, Muthassi?'

"'He is everywhere. If you concentrate, you might see him.'

"'See him?' I would ask eagerly. 'Have you seen him, Muthassi?'

"'I? I am not so fortunate, child. But I've heard Patteripad[5] say, when he read the *Bhagavatham*, that he and others like him have seen him, with his yellow silk, his peacock feathers, his flute. Sri Krishna! Hari Krishna! Krishna, Krishna!'

"Muthassi would close her eyes in an ecstasy of devotion, her trembling fingers working on the beads of her *japamala*. One would think she was looking directly at Bhagavan. I did not care for the stories about Patteripad and his reading sessions, but I felt a deep love for Sri Krishna. Which young girl could resist falling in love with this cowherd boy who danced and sang?

"It was my responsibility to arrange everything for the daily worship of the deity at the *illam*. I had to get up at dawn, have a bath, and string flower garlands. I had to light the lamp and do the abhishekam for the deities. Of the hundreds of images, the one I liked best was the statue of Vishnu, standing with Lakshmi. The very personification of love, he smiled as he held the Devi to his heart with the same hands that wielded the conch and disc. There was something in his expression that roused me. I would clean and polish the image every day and garland it. I would place a thilakam on its forehead. All the adornments I had loved and lost found their way into that place of worship. Yet, sometimes, at dawn or dusk, during those dreamlike hours filled with the fragrance of flowers, hot with incense and lamplight, when I knelt before the image of a god whose every limb was so infinitely beautiful, a faint desire would trouble me. Might I not wear even the garland that had been used for worship the day before and was now to be thrown away? Might I not place a sandalwood mark on my forehead? No, I might not. I might smear nothing on my forehead except the burnt ash of my desires.

"Muthassi's thoughts were for me, even as she drew her last breath, 'Unni, son, look after the child, she's so very young.' No one realized that destiny spoke those words through her. But a sense of danger menaced me. What could happen to a timid, blameless person like me?

" Time passed swiftly, but I did not realize that I was growing up. The days went by punctuated by rituals of bath and worship, the chanting of prayers. Truly, I never thought about myself until my older brother got married and brought his wife home. Why did that sister-in-law have to be so lovely? Why did the two of them suddenly break into loud laughter? She would have a bath every evening and put jasmine flowers in her hair. How beautifully she would pleat her *mundu* with its border of gold thread. A way of life which I had never known was being lived before my eyes. Every night, when the sound of those doors being closed fell upon my ears—do not be angry with me! I speak out of my sorrow. I am not envious of anyone. But when I think of how vastly experiences can differ, my heart breaks. After all, she was only six months older than me. A widow fears laughter and enjoyment more than tears. No matter whose it is, it hurts her. To stand and watch while the pleasures of life forever denied her are being experienced by another—do you know, you great vaidikans, how deeply that can hurt and sting?

"It is the fire fueled by this pain that smolders in the *antahpuram* of namboodiri houses. My sister-in-law provoked me continually. I could no longer find a single flower for the prayers on my favorite jasmine bush. The very first bud of the champakam tree that I had tended with infinite care was missing. Unable to control my grief and jealousy, I muttered, 'Which enchantress steals the flowers for my god to adorn herself? It wasn't for this that I tended my plants—'

"'What are flowers meant for if not for women blessed with the happiness of married life? There's no need for you to be so upset and talk like that, just because you can't have them yourself. Do you understand?'

"Her answer wounded me deeply. The seeds of domestic enmity had been sown. We quarreled over the most trivial things. We cried, scolded, and cursed each other. I always won. That's the way things are as long as one's parents are alive. My defeated sister-in-law would grind her teeth and mutter, 'All right—someday, I'll have an opportunity to pay you back. Till then—'

"I have learnt how cruelly such vengeful thoughts find their mark. Maybe I have endured more pain than they could ever inflict. All you namboodiris know the status of women born in our households. Most of the time, we have to live with our parents, because our husbands find it difficult to take care of their own families and cannot afford to look after us. We know no sorrow as long as our parents are alive. Indeed, we are even able to intimidate the women who have married into our households. But things change when the father dies and his younger brother takes charge. After that, only those who subordinate themselves to his wife and children have a comfortable existence. Orphans like us run here and there, victims of kitchen quarrels of the meanest kind. Even a servant who cleans the floors can get us into trouble, tell convincing lies about us, or scold us. I saw and suffered it all. I left the house in tears during the period of mourning for my mother's death.

"My husband's three marriages had left seven or eight daughters, who had all come of age, and were waiting to get married. Four of these daughters were older than me, and there were about ten children as well. I joined them. The old, leaking, dilapidated house echoed with cries of hunger and distress, but there was no one to listen to them. Maybe we were all expected to fend for ourselves. And yet, there was an advantage in being there—it was my own illam. No one could ask me to leave, and if someone did, I did not have to obey.

"My heart had hardened by now, and the jibes of my husband's other wives could not wound it. I could speak barbed words too. I had no children, nor any other responsibilities. A childless widow knows no tenderness. We live. We are doomed to live because we cannot die.

"I observed all the prescribed fasts. I worshipped at every shrine where a lamp was lit. I went without food for periods of fifteen days at a stretch. People spoke of me in those days as the ascetic of Thekkedath Illam. How soon all that has changed! Maybe you will accuse me of being a fraud. Go ahead then, mock me as much as you please. But let me ask you something. Have you, guardians of chastity and of the path of virtue, have you ever lifted a finger to protect pitiful creatures like us who have not even learned what life is all about? Destiny has decided that this world is not for us, and so we wander from door to door, seeking the peace and quiet that they say can be found at least in the other world. We struggle with desires we cannot suppress, sensations we cannot control, which are like steps slimy with the scum of sensual pleasure. If we stumble ever so slightly on these steps, you vaidikans and *smartans* submit us to cruel questions, punish us by throwing us into a pit of hell so deep that its borders cannot even be glimpsed from within it. Ah, God! Can Guruvayurappan or Vadakkunnathan, can our Ekadashi and Pradosham fasts help us in such a situation?"

A hot breeze blew through the opening in the door—or was it a stifled sigh? The assembly of vaidikans looked on in mute indifference. Was there no shred of humanity in them? No one spoke. After a pause, the accused continued her defense with greater firmness than before.

"I blame no one. This is my fate. After all, so many anterjanams go and listen to the Bhagavatham being read. Nothing happens to any of them. We used to have a reading of the Bhagavatham every year in our temple. Many anterjanams went to hear it, not merely out of devotion, or from the desire to listen to Bhagavan's stories. We went because we longed so much to go out, even with our umbrellas and shawls, because we wanted to experience the pleasure of listening to a male voice, even if we had to remain unseen. And, of course, we would earn our salvation through hearing the old epics being read. As far as we anterjanams are concerned, reading and bhajan-singing sessions are occasions that offer us opportunities to go out without incurring anyone's displeasure. And so disappointed widows, frustrated co-wives, and eternal virgins all gather behind the granary door in the temple to share our tears, our heartaches, our sighs.

"Our house is adjacent to the temple well, which was very convenient. I would get up early, have a bath, finish my rituals and prayers and then wait for it to be time to go for the reading session. It was so inspiring, just as Muthassi used to describe it to me. 'When Meppathoor and swamis like him call out, Bhagavan appears before them. Think of it, child! How fortunate one must be to reach that stage in life. And how much more fortunate we must consider ourselves to be able to have such great people read to us.'

"Our reader was no ascetic, nor was he one of those old men who had taken to the way of bhakti because he had grown indifferent to pleasure. And yet, when he entered, freshly bathed, in a starched mundu, with a sandalwood mark on his forehead, carrying his book and stand, people would find themselves standing up. For his face had a spiritual glow. He would sit before the shining lamp, cross-legged. He must have been about thirty-five years old. He was fair-skinned, broad-chested, and well built. He wore a yellow silk cloth around his waist, and flowers from the worship were tucked behind his ear. At every stage of the reading, when he raised his head to explain the verses, the radiance of his eyes matched the glitter of the diamond studs in his ears.

"Every one of us anterjanams worshipped him as the true incarnation of Sri Krishna. There was such music, such wit, such eloquence in the way he read. A mother wept, listening to the pranks of the little golden Krishna of Ambady, for she had just lost a son. A grandmother shed tears of joy as she heard the episode of Brahma stealing the cows and of Krishna blessing the married Brahmin women who found them. 'Bhagavan! Sri Krishna! Bhaktavatsala!'

"The old and learned nodded their heads in delight. 'He's better than Vazhakunnam,[6] there's no doubt about it.'

"I was not very interested in the infant Krishna's pranks. What was so entertaining about the mischievous behavior of a little child? I did not have a child, nor would I ever have one. Then why pay attention to all this? I preferred to look at the reader rather than listen to him.

"And so we came to the Rasakreeda,[7] which, as you all know, is the most beautiful part of the Bhagavatham. As the crowd in the inner rooms increased, the reader's enthusiasm intensified. His eyes grew wide, his tongue came alive, he seemed transformed into Lord Krishna himself. The cowherd magician's way of stealing women's clothes seemed invested with meaning. He told us that Bhagavan played with a thousand *gopis* through the long dark nights in the forest on the banks of the Yamuna while others slept. He read each line, then expounded on its meaning. His vivid descriptions made virgins bow their heads in shyness, and wives smile. Widows sighed over old memories and murmured prayers. I had no hopes, no experiences, no memories. I could listen if I wished, idly, indifferently, and then allow everything I had heard to settle within me, so that I would be able to use the rewards of having listened, and the emotions I had felt while doing so, in some other life. And that was all.

"He recited a verse from the Gopika Gita[8] and explained it :'What a fortunate woman Radhika was. Did she not forsake her husband and children, forsake all her duties, to answer the call of the golden flute? Did she not delight in proclaiming that love was her salvation? Bhagavan! Guruvayurappan! Who understands the meaning of your frolic and play? Sin and salvation, justice and duty, are all illusions before your endless flow of music. We may forget the ten incarnations and all the other parts of Sri Krishna's story. But these fascinating scenes from Brindavanam will continue to plunge us in bliss for ages to come—'

"'Love is bhakti—love is moksha[9]—the bliss of love is the achievement of true communion with God.'

"I gazed steadily at that face, longing for some explanation beyond words. Love is moksha—love is bliss—what did it mean, the fulfillment of love?

"He sat in the auspicious circle of lamplight, the Bhagavatham open before him, his eyes half-closed, his palms joined in worship. He seemed the very personification of love. For an instant, his shining eyes looked into our room. It was only then that I realized that I was in the front row, at the door. Trembling, I pulled my head back. I experienced an astonishing emotion. Was it shyness, or modesty, or uneasiness? I was afraid. Would he have seen me? What a deformed creature I must appear, with my disheveled hair and wan cheeks.

"The son of one of the older wives of my husband had a little mirror. I took it secretly that evening, and looked into it. It was a long time since I had seen my face so clearly. Was there a faded beauty lurking in the sad reflection? Could it be likened to Radha's beautiful face, when she looked tired and sad with the grief of separation?

"The next morning, after my bath, I took care to comb my hair neatly. Instead of the usual holy ash, I placed a little mark on my forehead with sandalwood paste. I tucked a strand with the ten sacred flowers, freshly plucked, into my hair, took my umbrella and shawl, and went to the temple. Someone was chanting prayers in front of the outer hall, in a beautiful voice. I slanted my umbrella a little and looked out very cautiously to see who it was. He was looking at me. An uneasiness I had never felt before took hold of me. My legs trembled. My eyes misted. I returned home quickly, without completing the ritual of circling the temple.

"After that, whenever I went for the reading sessions, I took care to sit in the back row. I did not want to look anyone in the face. And yet, I could not stay away. To hear him speak those words, to sit close to where he was, gave me an unmistakable sense of comfort. Did I feel this way because of the greatness of the epic he read to us?

"I thought of nothing else, even while I ate or slept. I saw the banks of the Yamuna, the flowering kadamba, and Radha, mad with love. And the playful, romantic Bhagavan. Ah, whose form was this? The yellow silk, the diamond earrings, the smile—was this Bhagavan's true form? But then, Bhagavan could take any form.

"Throughout the month of Magha, I used to bathe in the temple tank every morning in the mist-filled dawn and go for the first worship of the day to the temple. This was a practice I had begun long ago. Someone had told me, when I was very young, that doing this would bring me fulfillment of my desires. I had no desires, but I performed the ritual regularly. Of late, I used to hear a song in the cool of the morning that made me shudder with delight. And there were ripples on the water. Someone must be having a bath, I thought, someone lonely like me.

"I know I had grown very weak emotionally, in the endless struggle with my illusory desires. Still, I can swear that I never once imagined the possibility of what actually happened.

"I mistook the dim shadows of the Makara moonlight for daybreak and hurried to the tank, forgetting even to ask my chaperone to come with me. All I could think of was that it would be dreadful if I missed the morning worship. In my haste to reach the temple, I had just immersed myself in the tank, and rapidly dried myself, when I heard a night bird screech in the asoka tree in the temple courtyard. A cool breeze blew, wafting the fragrance of midnight blossoms. As the full moon dipped lower into the western sky, the tall shadow of the tank behind me grew larger and fuller. Between the moonlight and the shadow lay the huge tank itself, like a woman's heart, silent with emotion.

"The readings I had listened to for many days seemed to have touched me with poetry. Would not those lovely nights on the banks of the Yamuna have been like this? With the Govardhan mountain on one side, carpeted in silky green, glowing in the moonlight, and a soft breeze playing joyfully in the thrill of the young spring . . . On the other side, the houses of the cowherds would lie wrapped in darkness, and hearts hardened by harsh lives would be quietened in sleep.

"Between these two very different scenes, the slow Kalindi River flowed like a dream, its limpid depths reflecting the dark blue sky and a million glimmering stars while lotuses and water lilies opened out gently on its surface. Centuries ago, the sweet, pure music of Krishna's flute had soared upward from the banks of this river. The echoes of that music have stayed with us through time, diffusing the nectar of hope even into withered hearts like mine.

"As I stood there lost in these thoughts, I involuntarily hummed a melody from an *ashtapadi* I had learned as a child. Human beings have an incurable weakness—on certain occasions, and in certain surroundings, the human mind cannot contain itself. Indeed, I am sure that even experts like you can be vulnerable like this. How then can you find fault with a woman like me? And yet, even in the half-conscious state that I was in, I was truly terrified when two hot arms encircled me. Who was this? Could it be Bhagavan himself? Lord, you have appeared thus so many times before your devotees.

"Startled awake from the world of imagination, my natural prudence asserted itself. 'No, it can't be. There can be no direct experience of God in the *kaliyuga*. Ayyo! Then who else could it be?'

"A cry arose from the depths of my being, but it was smothered by a gentle kiss. A futile writhing, and I had perforce to yield to a strong embrace. In the surge of sensations my resistance ebbed away. Feelings of pleasure that I had never known or experienced before came alive.

"Or had I become weak, was I going to faint? It seemed to me that this was no dream, nor indeed was it sleep. Like everyone else, I too had to admit defeat in the struggle against my natural instincts. If that is a sin, I will sell my soul for it."

"Do not ask whether that encounter ever recurred. Nor try to find out who that god was. I am guilty. You can punish me. No one else shares my guilt."

1940

NOTES

1. Since a smartavicharan is a trial of a person accused of transgressing the laws of a community, the defendant is depleted of human status as a social being and referred to as a "thing" (sadhanam) and kept in isolation in a building outside the main living quarters.
2. Magha is a sacred period corresponding to the Malayalam month of Kumbham. Ritual baths taken during this month are said to cleanse one of all sins; eating only one meal a day during the month of Vaisakha is supposed to ensure happiness in marriage. Other rites of Vaisakha include early morning baths, going to the temple and receiving the sacred water.

3. Refers to the sambandham system of the nairs. See Introduction, p.xv.
4. Women wore the mangalyasutram on a thread around their necks as a sign of marriage. They held this thread in their hands while reciting mantrams that would ensure them long married lives.
5. The sixteenth-century poet-devotee Melpathur Narayana Bhattadiripad, author of the Sanskrit work on Krishna, the *Narayaneeyam*.
6. Vazhakunnam Neelakantan Namboodiri (1903-1959), a well-known magician. His skill was legendary in Kerala.
7. A part of the Bhagavatham, the story of Krishna, which deals with the romantic episodes of Krishna and the gopikas.
8. The song sung by the gopikas to express their grief at being separated from Krishna; a part of the Bhagavatham.
9. Hindu belief in the reunion of the soul with God and thus freedom from rebirth.

Within the Folds of Seclusion

MOODUPADATHIL 5

THE MOODUPADAM[1] that covered her was very thick. What might the form under it be like? Young or old? Beautiful or deformed? Soft or shriveled and dried up? There was no trace of a clue that might betray its likeness. It slept peacefully on a bed of dried darbha grass.[2] The light from a brass oil lamp flickered against the darkness with a fearsome glow.

It was profoundly quiet and the silence terrified me. I couldn't bear to think of breaking such a stillness with even a sigh.

While she was alive, she had never really looked at the world around her. She had hated noise. However loud her heartbeats were, she had suppressed them because she did not want others to hear them. Why, I thought, should we disturb her now with an account of her experiences that she herself would never have wanted to give?

Relief, satisfaction, peace—feelings she had never experienced in life—she had them all now. Cruelty would no longer make her weep, nor rebukes hurt her. The authority of others would not smother her anymore. She had found peace and complete freedom. Sleep, my sister, sleep happily. I know that this is the first time you have ever been able to rest quietly.

People whispered in the next room. As part of the ritual, they sobbed and shed tears which, however, did not touch their hearts. They had never spoken a kind word to her when she was alive. Now, they were full of praise for her, "Pappi is fortunate. She was still wearing her *thali* when she died."

A mango tree was being cut down in the southern courtyard. A pit had already been dug close to it. They were preparing to perform the last rites. Everyone looked as if a burden had been lifted from them. There was a sense of relief and contentment, the kind that was generally seen only in a house where a girl had just been married off.

Why then did I feel so distressed? Who had she been to me, the young woman who had achieved freedom at last? She had not been really close to me. She was only a neighbor, someone I knew. We might have been distantly related. But what did a relationship mean? Was it limited to worldly ties, to family connections? Were not those whose souls and feelings drew them together also related to each other? If they were, then no two people in the world were as closely related as this young woman and I. But only the two of us knew this. And now, only I did.

She had revealed the depths of her tender heart to me, its deep wounds, its torments and sorrows. And its memories, both happy and painful, which she had guarded closely and no one knew about.

Forgive me, my sister. I know I do not have your permission to speak of these things and that even at this moment you will not excuse me for doing so. But I cannot help recalling that pitiful story once more as thousands of emotions batter my heart. It will not harm you; it will only lead you to a purer world, cleansed of evil.

A woman's heart has secrets that even the funeral pyre cannot reveal. Suppressed continually by the opposing forces of religion, society, even destiny, they finally explode within her. Like weeping without tears, living without breathing, like a mountain of fire that cannot give out smoke, they are contained inside her and shatter her inner being.

She was an innocent child, half-crazy. No one guessed the conflict in her heart, no one knew what it was that caused her to die young. Pappi was not yet twenty-five when she died.

She had been brought to her husband's house as a bride one

day in mid-Edavam, during the heavy monsoon rains. There were no ululations or decorations to welcome her, and not even a lamp had been lit to receive her. When their old namboodiri husband, who had gone to Thirunavaya, came back one night with a fourth wife, the three other wives scowled at her from the inner rooms. The sounds of a fierce gale, of thunder, and torrential rain were the festive music that greeted her arrival.

Selfishness is an innate part of us. Woman or man, young or old, educated or illiterate, everyone falls victim to it. How can they be blamed? Her older sisters—her husband's other wives—had good reason to be afraid. She was beautiful and young. They were sure that she would exert a great influence over her sixty-year-old husband.

Astonishingly, this did not happen. Pappi ignored her husband totally. She did not look after him, nor would she go to him if he called her. They counseled, scolded, punished, and even ill-treated her, but it was no use. She was as unmoved as a stone. People began to whisper about her, "She's a terrible woman. He might be old and ugly, but he's her husband, her god in this life. Why doesn't she love and worship him? Why doesn't she compete with the other wives to do so?"

Pappi would not answer their questions. She spoke to no one and wanted no one to speak to her. She bathed early every morning, entered the kitchen, and stayed there till midnight. She refused to comb her hair, or place a sandalwood mark on her forehead. No one ever saw her laugh. It was a strange way for a newly married girl to behave! The other wives muttered, "The wretch! Who knows where he found her."

Pappi could easily have governed her husband if she wanted to, and revenged herself on the other wives. But she did not care to do this. She hated his looks, his voice, his very proximity.

She would sometimes gaze into the distance as if dreaming of something unattainable, something she had lost and would never find again. Or she would stand holding the kitchen ladle for hours together, not moving.

She often sat in the courtyard at night, on the little platform where a jasmine grew, and looked at the star-filled sky, sobbing bitterly; no one knew why. She seemed to live in another world, distanced from her immediate surroundings. Was there someone in that world who would weep with her?

The rumor spread that the new *anterjanam* at Puthillam was mad. In the beginning, I believed this.

I remember very clearly the unforgettable day when you dispelled my misconceptions, Pappi, when you moved aside the moodupadam that hid your secret and showed me the heartrending picture of your life. I have thought often of that day. What a great burden you had taken upon yourself. The battle between your own desires and rigid customs; the conflict between emotions and beliefs; all the hairsplitting arguments that have always confronted women over the years—you did not fail the test they imposed. But you did not win either. The conflict made you mad. Or rather, they decided you were mad because they did not understand you. You became silent and indifferent, as if you had withdrawn from life. The day you spoke to me, you unknowingly transferred a part of your burden to my shoulders. And now that intolerable burden is completely mine to bear, for you have left your cage to soar free and unfettered into the infinite.

What a night that was! It was Sivaratri,[3] the sacred night that awakens the purest emotions in the hearts of devotees all over Hindu India and brings them peace filled with thoughts of Siva. Groups of people gathered in temples and houses, fasted, and kept awake through the night. They sang songs, prayed, and told each other stories.

The Anterjanam Samajam had arranged to meet in her *illam* that day. I did not usually enjoy such gatherings, and only took part in them to be polite. Of course, I knew I could pick up bits and pieces for the plots of my stories from the women's endless chatter.

The meeting continued until well after nine. I looked out. It was a quiet lovely night. The Goddess of Nature seemed to have veiled herself in the black darkness of the new moon night. Innumerable tears glinted in the wide expanse of the sky, with no one to wipe them away. The summer breeze was laden with the intoxicating fragrance of the kuvalam. Fireworks could be heard from the temple, and the sound of a conch. Caught in the excitement of the festival, people cried out, "Hara! Hara! Mahadeva!"

As if in answer, the tired voices of the women who were fasting rose from the inner room:

> "Born on this earth, a human being,
> I am adrift in this sea of hell.
> Take me ashore from this hell . . ."

It was such a sorrowful lament. Although I had heard this folk-song about the deity of the Vaikkam temple a thousand times, it seemed to have a special strength and meaning now as it soared into the dark night, sung by women who had fasted for days and who lived in the kind of hell the words described. Generations of women had sung the song, and yet what had they gained?

Humming the song as I walked in the courtyard I changed the words of the last line to

> "We shall climb ashore from this hell."

Suddenly, I heard someone crying softly. I looked around and saw a woman's form near the jasmine bush. I knew at once who it was. It was the young woman, the mad woman who never smiled, never spoke to anyone. Some inner force urged me to approach her. She was lost in thought and looked as if some great sorrow weighed her down. I felt very sad. I thought she's not really mad. A deep sense of hopelessness must have made her like that.

"Pappi!" I placed my hand on her shoulder. Startled by my unexpected touch, she scrambled to her feet.

"Who is it? Edathi . . . I didn't think—" She seemed surprised. After all, I had never spoken to her with affection. No one had.

"Why have you come out alone in the dark, Edathi?" She asked.

"Why are you sitting alone in the dark?" I countered.

"I often do this. And, especially, today—" She seemed distressed. "I like to be by myself."

"And I must try and comfort people who are crying."

"How can human beings prevent each other from crying, Edathi? We have to endure our destinies."

"That's not right," I said. "We make or mar our own destinies. What makes you so sad, Pappi? However great your sorrow is, it will help if you share it."

She raised her head and looked at me doubtfully. I think she was not certain whether I really cared, and whether she could trust me. Her cheeks were flushed, her eyes reddened with crying, and her hair disheveled. Her face was beautiful, though full of pain.

"Pappi," I called eagerly, "tell me the truth. I know you're not mad."

"No," she said in a firm voice, "I've never been mad."

"Then why do you pretend you are?"

"I don't know why people treat me as if I'm mad."

"Don't you know? It's because you cry all the time. And you don't care for your husband."

"Husband, indeed!" She shuddered. "Who is this person you call a husband?"

"The one you marry with fire as witness. That's what our society says."

Pappi was silent for a long time. She seemed deeply troubled. I stroked her back gently and said, "Don't cry, Pappi. I won't ask you anything if you don't want me to. And I'll go away if you don't want me to stay. Please don't cry."

"No, no, Edathi, I want to tell you. I will tell you." She went on firmly, "Is it not a sin for a woman who has already touched a man to become the wife of another? Is it not a violation of the law of chastity?"

I was astonished. What a question! I had never heard of a namboodiri woman asking such a question. Yes, it was a violation of the law of chastity and a sin for a young girl who had not only looked at but also touched a man before her marriage, to become another man's wife. Ethics, customs, priests would all consider her, and her lover, fallen. I could not think of an answer. She waited for some time, then said, with great disappointment, "That's what I meant, Edathi. It's my fate, it is bound to happen. I'll tell you my story."

"It happened on a Sivaratri night like this one. My mother and I were fasting. Father had gone to the temple, and his younger brother was visiting his wife's family. Our neighbors were all at the temple for the festival. Amma had her head buried in the *Siva Puranam* and I could hear our old servant woman mumbling her prayers in the northern block of the house. It was very hot inside. I could not sleep. So I opened the door and slipped out quietly. Through the banana trees and palms I could see the flares of the pronged torches and oil lamps in the temple and hear the indistinct murmur of the crowd.

"As children, we had often watched the festival, sitting by the jasmine bower. Whom do I mean by 'we'? Don't ask me that. Unmarried women are often afraid to explore their own dreams. I stayed where I was, immersed in my thoughts, my indefinable hopes and desires.

"Suddenly, I heard a footstep behind me and got up, confused, just as I did when I saw you today. I thought it was Achan or Amma, and I turned, ready to be scolded. But it was someone else. There are people one can recognize even when it is pitch dark. It was a man, Edathi, a man I knew!

"I think he too was confused by the unexpectedness of the encounter. Our eyes met for a moment. I was on the point of running inside, but my feet were numb, I don't know why. After a while, he said, 'Pappi.'

"Never in my life had anyone called my name with so much tenderness and feeling.

"'Have you forgotten me, Pappi? Are you annoyed with me?'

"What could I say? Forget him! My Ettan, my playmate, my father's nephew. We had played together as children, grown up and gone to school together. We often playfully pinched and slapped each other in those days. I was never upset, no matter what he did, for I had heard Amma say, 'Kuttan is going to marry Pappi.' If a husband slapped his wife, she must endure it and even take pleasure in it, I thought. And so that happy time went by. Once he had learned to recite the Vedas, he went away to study. I came of age and was shut up in the *antahpuram*. We had not seen each other for five years now.

"That morning, Father had called out to me,'Pappi, make Kuttan some coffee.' I had forgotten how tired I was from fasting and had peered excitedly at him through the slats of the wooden door.

"And here he was now, asking whether I had forgotten him after five long years of separation!

"I could not hold back my tears. 'Who forgot whom?' I asked, my voice full of reproach. He could have come as often as he wanted. He was a man, after all, and men could do what they liked, go where they wanted.

"He came close to me and said, smiling, 'Forget you! It would be easier to forget myself. Neither of us has the strength to forget each other, Pappi. We never will.'

"'Then all this time—' I broke down. He could not bear it. He reached out to touch me. He might have thought I was going to fall down and wanted to support me, or maybe he caressed me because I was trembling. Whatever it was, Edathi, I could not push him away. I went limp.

"I wept in his arms till I could weep no more. I felt his tears fall on my head. There are moments, Edathi, when we forget ourselves. I did not protest when he lifted my head. The stars looked down at us. The earth and sky are my witnesses, I swear by God that it was he who bent his face to mine.

"As children, we had often kissed each other fearlessly.

"When I realized where I was, I broke free and ran. What would happen, I asked myself, if anyone came to know of this union of a young namboodiri girl and a young man who was not her husband? My God! My heart throbbed with fear, and my body trembled. Would Amma be awake?

"The lamps in the prayer room burned low. I saw the divine image of Siva with Parvathi on his lap. I had decorated it with flowers that morning. My Lord, I asked, don't you know what has happened?

"Trembling violently, like a child who has done something wrong, I knelt and prostrated myself. Lord Vadakkunnathan! I prayed, forgive me this time. Please don't let anyone know!

"I've forgotten how long I lay there. I realized it was morning only when Amma came and shook me.

"Ettan left that day. I've never seen him since and no one knows what happened between us. I live for the memory of that moment, that event. It comforts me, but it makes me mad as well."

She stopped speaking. A bee droned amongst the jasmine flowers. A few blossoms fell in the gentle breeze. A pair of owls quarreled with each other in a tree some distance away.

I asked, "Then he didn't come back? Did they never think of him as a possible husband for you?"

She sounded very sad. "No, Edathi, it did not happen that way. That's why I said fate willed it so. For a long time, I had no news of him. One day, I heard father say to someone, 'That scoundrel Kuttan has cut off his tuft[4] and eats with people of other castes. They say he's joined the Congress and is in jail now.'

"I understood why he never came home. Father would never consider my marrying a man who had been cast out of the community! They considered many proposals of marriage for me. But the dowry we could afford never matched the prestige of the family in question. I lived in constant fear that they would find me a husband. How would I look at his face or hold his hand? My God, I prayed, take my life away before that happens!

"And then, unfortunately, my father died. His younger brother, who took charge of the household, was more interested in his wife's family than ours. Although Amma wept and pleaded, the question of my marriage was neglected. I hoped Ettan would come out of jail one day and remember me. I was prepared to leave everything, Edathi, and run away with him. But why talk of that? One night, my father's brother, who had gone to Thirunavaya, came back earlier than expected. We assumed that the old man he had brought with him was a visitor. I realized the truth only when Amma came to me in the morning with henna and a silver ring. There was no way out, no chance to run away or to commit suicide.

"And so my marriage took place since there were no obstacles to prevent it. My heart, my hopes, my life itself was thrown into the smoldering *homam* fire and burned to cinders. But I did not weep. I said nothing. I endured it all, my heart as hard as a stone. When my husband took my hand in his old, shriveled one, my father's brother was triumphant. Could anyone else, he asked, have conducted a marriage for five hundred rupees?

"However, the marriage was not consummated. The old man was not as strong as I was. The pretence of madness has become my defense. But I cannot forget that night, and that other person, no matter how hard I try. It is a sin, isn't it, for a married woman to think of another man? A violation of her chastity?"

As she came to the end of her story, she looked at me as anxiously as a lawyer might look at the judge after he has made his defense. What could I say?

"Man has always made the rules of dharma to suit himself," I said, "and we have never had the right to question them. But I am sure that it cannot be wrong for you to think of that event, even of him, if it gives you comfort. However, I don't think you should continue to stay here. Go back to the house where you were born and try to believe that this marriage never existed. The rest is up to you. I can't say more."

The morning star peered out of the leaves of the tree in the east. A cock crowed. I could hear people laugh and talk loudly as they came back from the temple. It had grown bright. We got up.

Pappi went back to the house where she was born. I heard that she was cured of her madness, and that she was happy. May her bruised heart know a little happiness, I prayed.

The next five or six years were uneventful as far as I was concerned. The most important years of a woman's life are when she is between sixteen and thirty. She is nature's partner in the process of creation and it is for her to impart growth and vivacity to the world of the future. Immersed in my endless round of duties, I forgot Pappi and her sad story.

One evening, when I was hurriedly writing something in my room, a servant came up to me and said, "Pappi Kunhathol[5] has come back to Puthillam. She's very ill and wants to see you."

I was surprised. Why had she returned after such a long time? How could she have fallen so seriously ill? What did it mean?

Pappi's symptoms had been peculiar. She had refused to eat or drink, or get up from bed. She had insisted that she was going to die, and that she wanted to die in her husband's house. They had brought her back by boat, an emaciated bag of bones. Why had she wanted to come back to a place she had abandoned, only to die there?

Pappi lay in a dark room. The women outside whispered to me, "She might last through the night, that's all."

I sat beside her and wiped away my tears. Holding her long thin hands in mine, I called softly, "Pappi?"

She opened her eyes and looked at me with great sadness. "Edathi." Her voice trembled. Both of us wept, like sisters born of one flesh, one mother.

I tried to comfort her. "Don't worry, Pappi, you'll soon be better."

"Yes, I'll soon be better, Edathi. I wanted to see you all before I was cured, that's why I came." She continued thoughtfully, "I am not sorry. It's better to die than be killed by degrees."

We both knew that she had something important to say. But I did not have the courage to ask, nor she to speak. She was silent for a while, then she said tiredly, "I saw him again, Edathi, that proud social reformer, the Congressman I had dreamed of and waited for. He had repented of his sins. He now has a sambandham[6] with my father's brother's daughter. They walk in the courtyard every night and sing. They are so happy, so much in love! I could not bear it, Edathi! I did not want to die in that house. After all, this is my house, for my husband is here, isn't he?"

Who was her husband?

She laid her head on the old man's feet as she was dying and begged his forgiveness,

"Bear with me, pardon my sins. Grant me peace at least in the next world."

He wept as bitterly as she did.

And so her pure soul dissolved into eternal rest in peace and calmness.

Do not remove her moodupadam or try to look behind it. Do not disturb her with even the softest of sighs. Let the poor young woman sleep peacefully.

1940

NOTES

1. The length of unbleached cloth with which the woman's face and body were covered. It was considered unpolluted and was therefore used during rituals.
2. When death approached, namboodiris were laid on the ground on a layer of sand covered by a layer of darbha grass. It was considered auspicious for the dying to draw the last three breaths in this position.
3. A festival held in the month of Kumbham in which Siva is worshipped by married women and unmarried girls seeking long, happy married lives.
4. Male namboodiris had their hair cut so that a tuft would remain hanging; to cut off the tuft would be a break with tradition.
5. Young Athol, a form of address for anterjanams.
6. See Introduction, p.xv.

Wooden Cradles

MARATHOTTIL   6

T HESE ARE events that took place a long time ago, events that
go as far back as the memory of a thirty-year-old woman can
take her. You all know how much a little child between the
ages of three and nine, especially a little girl, delights in listening
to someone telling old legends. And if she has an old woman servant at her command, her happiness is complete. She asks a thousand questions, and must be given reasons for everything that
happens. Whom does the kitchen cat call out to when it mews all
the time? Why are the cat and the dog at each other's throats? Is
it because they are brothers? When the mother sparrow goes out
from the nest every morning in search of food, aren't the baby
sparrows afraid to be by themselves? Doesn't the sky mother get
furious when her children overturn her box of vermilion every day,
morning and evening? And so they sprout, endlessly, the young
tendrils of curiosity.

The cherished darling of a wealthy family can exercise many
unjust privileges over the servants in the household. She will ride
nothing but a human horse. She must be told a dozen stories before
she will drink a glass of milk. At the end of a crowded day, if she
must desist from further mischief and go to sleep, her old slave
must sing every song she knows.

Uncle Moon was exhausted, for he had been wandering all day in search of food for his starving wife and children. At last, by dusk, he had found a handful of broken rice grains. On his way home across the vast sky, he slipped, and the rice grains scattered and became stars!

The little one interrupts to ask innocently, "And are the children still crying for food?"

When the sky turns dark, when lightning flashes and thunder roars, we know that the Lord of the Skies is preparing for war. The Great One, the Sun, set out in his royal chariot to marry the daughter of the Lord of the Skies. A demon stopped him on the way and would not let him go on. The Lord of the Skies whirled his sword. The thunder you hear is the demon roaring in pain. And the raindrops you see are the tears of the bride and her attendants, distraught with the fear that the wedding will never take place.

Infant logic must clear a doubt, "And did the wedding take place?"

We all learned our first lessons in life from such women. It was forbidden to swim in the tank next door because two people once drowned in it; if little girls went out to play under the elanji tree, a yakshi[1] would tear them to pieces; if you played with your shadow, you would be born a demon in your next life. As we approach the last stage of childhood, these old women begin to seem as useless to us as antiquated wooden cradles. Their hands suddenly feel coarse and rough. And yet, the crude images that those roughened nails once etched on the tender walls of a child's mind continue to gleam fitfully beneath the veneer of time, now clear, now indistinct.

Once I was thirteen, I had no time for Nangelipennu. Her house was a good ten miles from ours. She had come to us when she was eleven years old, when my father was still a child. She had lived with us, a part of the family, for sixty-two years, till she was old and helpless. No one in her family had cared to arrange a match for her, so she had never married. Although she was unmarried, she always had children whom she could call her own. Their jewels were hers and their toys too. She shared their illnesses and all their pleasures. One by one, each child in the family became her charge. As she relinquished each little one who had learned to walk on its own, another newborn was placed in her arms. She would hold it close and proudly chant:

"God gave this little baby
To parents who longed for one.
God gave this little baby
To Nangeli who longed for one."

She had sung generations of babies to sleep with her cradle songs, her affection flowing generously from father to daughter, uncle to nephew. Every child in the family grew up under her care. And yet, when she fell seriously ill in her seventy-third year with rheumatic pains and chills, our foster mother had no home that she could call her own.

When Nangelipennu left us, my youngest brother, the eighth in the family, was three years old. She bathed him, placed a *thilakam* on his forehead, dressed him in a silk shirt and trousers, and kissed him, her eyes full of tears. "Who will be Nangelipennu's baby now?"

He was my mother's last child. There would be no more babies in the *tarawad*. Nangelipennu was old and sick now and she no longer wanted to stay in a house where the other servants jeered at her. She was far too proud to stay where she was not needed. All the same, she was unutterably sad when she said goodbye to us. She kissed each of us children in turn and then asked me, in a voice choked with tears, "Will you think of me, child, when you're married and living happily with your husband? I'll come for your wedding."

I was furious. I hated anyone talking to me about marriage. Two of my younger aunts had recently been married, and both had left the house weeping. They seldom came home now. Who would look after my flower pots, my pictures, my cupboard, my books, if I went away as they had done?

"In that case," I said gruffly to Nangelipennu, "you need never come back." And I moved away from her.

She often asked my eleven-year-old brother, "When you've got your B.A. and all, what will you give Nangelipennu?" He detested her, would never go to her. "Get away from me! You'll stain my clothes with your snot!" In the end, Nangelipennu realized what had happened—all the little ones whom she had hatched in the loving warmth of her hands had become birds that soared in the skies. They would find tall trees to build nests in, they would revel in the wide firmament. They would never come back to the little nests of broken twigs they once had been content with.

One of Nangelipennu's distant relatives had a granddaughter who had a baby every year. She couldn't go out to work because of the little ones. Nangeli Amma arrived and took charge. Over the next four years, she had the good fortune to have five babies to care for. None of the children wanted their mother, they preferred their new grandmother.

The years went by. Despite all my protests, I had to give in and get married. Nangelipennu did not come to my wedding. Instead, her granddaughter brought us the news, "It started with a fever and a chill. She didn't even last two hours. Oh, Amme, the little one is still crying. She refuses to eat because she wants her grand-mother."

In time, I had a baby too. I hunted everywhere for a live wooden cradle that would keep my child away from fire and water, calm him when he cried, and look after him with care. The memory of Nangelipennu came alive again and touched my heart. The old servant had been dead for years now. No one like her could be found in our part of the country. Her granddaughter had her own children and grandchildren to look after. Indeed, all the mothers and grandmothers I knew had children of their own to care for.

After a long and arduous search, I found someone named Bhanumathi. She was fourteen, had never handled babies before, and was herself a child. When the baby cried, she would not come anywhere near him. And, anyway, it would have been no use if she did, the baby burst into tears every time he saw her cross face.

I caught myself remembering the innumerable ways in which Nangelipennu used to coax a fractious child into good humor again. She would twist her lips in an expression of reproach, widen her eyes, hold out her arms, and say, "Did you hear the drums, little one? There he comes, the kavadi[2] man.

"With a young moon in his hair
He comes, on a blue peacock,
Velavan, my savior!
Haraharo! Hara!"

"If you don't come with me, little one, Nangelipennu will go off by herself." Which child could resist her invitation?

From our upstairs window, we could see the Nagamala range, enveloped in clouds. Two strange rock formations that looked like demons covered in smoke lay between two of its peaks. They were known as "Pandi" and "Pandiyathi." Whenever a child cried, Nangelipennu would say, "Look at Pandi and Pandiyathi. God turned them into rocks because they were obstinate and willful."

The most disobedient child would give in to this threat, for no one wanted to turn into a rock that could not move. And then, of course, Nangelipennu had to repeat the oft-told story once more, with new embellishments. She would sit on the floor, her legs outstretched, eager to start, and the children would crowd around her, their eyes wide with delight saying "Tell us, how did Pandi and Pandiyathi turn into rocks?"

Drumming gently on her knees, the old storyteller would begin:

"Once upon a time, in the kingdom of Pandi, there lived a king and a queen. The king had a gold chariot that took him wherever he wanted to go, and the queen had a gold chain that gave her whatever she wished for. One day they came to hunt in Nagamala.

"The king, tired and thirsty after a long day's hunting, sat down on a rock. There was not a drop of water anywhere near. He prayed, 'Lord of Nagamala, if a pond appears here now, I'll make you a handsome offering.'

"Amazing! A spring gurgled toward them from the top of the mountain. They took a handful of water in the hollow of their hands and drank, and their hunger and thirst were quenched.

"The exhausted queen prayed, 'Lord of the Mountain! If you build me a palace here, I too will make you a worthy offering.'

"Astonishing! A seven-story mansion appeared magically. Its floor was of gold, its walls of precious gems. The king and the queen slept in it and woke up on the third day. They were loath to leave. The king said, 'If I sell the entire Pandi kingdom, I'll never have as much gold as there is here. Let's take as much as we can in our chariot.'

"The queen said, 'I'll not find a single gem as lovely as these in the whole treasury. I must have one for my chain.'

"Disgusted with their cupidity, God decided to punish them. 'You can stay here forever and enjoy the gold and the gems.' And he turned them both into rocks. So you see, my children, how evil greed can be."

These grandmother's tales, which have their origin in superstitions, stay long in our minds, complete with a moral that is related to life. But the women who narrated them, women like Nangelipennu, are no more. Today's children no longer have old-fashioned wooden cradles, they have pretty bunched ones of fine net. Old sweet country songs have been forgotten and recorded music has taken their place. But the heart of a child does not change. One day, when thunder roared and rain swished down, my son asked me, "What is that thudding on the roof, Amme?"

I knew what it was: sea water becomes water vapor, rises, cools, and falls as rain. When clouds collide, sparks of electricity are ignited, and there is lightning and thunder. I knew, but all the same, I said to him, "It is the Lord of the Skies making ready for war."

1941

NOTES

1. A demigoddess or spirit.
2. Shaped like a wooden bow, decorated with peacock feathers and flowers, this object is carried by pilgrims to the Subramania temple.

The Devi and Her Devotee

DEVIYUM ARADHAKANUM

T HE DOOR OF THE *garbhagriha* was closed for the worship with lamps. The sound of the conch filled the air. The soft chant of mantrams mingled with the peal of holy bells somewhere in the inner precincts of the temple. It was like a dream world, something that the eyes could hardly contain. "Devi! Mahamaye!" Devotees thronged at the door so that they could offer worship as soon as it opened to show them the divinely auspicious image. In the transcendental peace of the dusk, the bells at the entrance rang ceaselessly.

The door of the garbhagriha suddenly opened before the crowd of silent worshippers. The image of the virgin goddess shone among masses of flowers and thousands of little glowing lamps strung in chains. She held a wedding garland in her golden hands. The holy eyes, filled with a lover's radiant hopes, were touched with the faintest shadow of tender impatience, as she waited in the marriage hall for the bridegroom who had not yet arrived. A fragrant breeze laden with the scent of sandalwood sticks and incense flowed toward the entrance like divine breath. The senses rose above the consciousness of the self in an ecstasy of *bhakti*. Even the bells, which had been ringing continuously, stopped for a moment as if the very heart of the universe was stilled. It was like the heaven of perfect nirvana.

The priest stood at the door, his *mundu* taken between his legs and tucked in at the back in ritual fashion, a tulasi garland around his neck, looking like an embodiment of the noblest human qualities. He held a platter blazing with flames, and a silver *kindi* that contained *thirtham,* and he also offered *prasadam.* People flocked eagerly toward him. It is in the nature of human beings to compete with one another even in the presence of God. The priest gazed at them with compassion. Was there anyone, he wondered, among these devotees who really merited a blessing?

There was a gentle murmur in the crowd. A lovely girl poised between childhood and youth came forward slowly. As her white silk saree swirled around her feet, the gold stripes on its border gleamed brightly. She held a small leaf cup filled with freshly opened champakam flowers in her hand. People moved aside respectfully. She looked like the daughter of an aristocratic family, anyone would have made way for her.

She placed the flowers at the door, joined her palms, and bowed low. How seductively beautiful she was! The glowing champakam flowers shone like gold, their colors strikingly like the tone of her skin. She made another obeisance, her timid eyes full of appeal. Astonishing! The dreamlike shadow of impatience was visible in her eyes as well! Some inexplicable emotion gave her cheeks the colour of vermilion.

The priest gazed at the image and the devotee in turn. He had never seen such a faithful likeness before. His eyes widened with pleasure. It was as if the rituals and the meditation he had performed over many days, as if all his dreams were at last being fulfilled. Where could human beings attain the presence of God if not in each other?

The flames on his platter were reflected in the half-dark of her eyes and from there into his own eyes. He held out the sacred lamp and as she extended her slender pale fingers to invoke the pure flame into her face, they gleamed like reddish petals.

He put down the platter and picked up the kindi and the offerings. She stretched out her hands respectfully. He poured the holy water into her hands, which were like a flower that bloomed with youthful desire, and his own hands trembled, he was not quite sure why.

The young man had been a priest now for more than five years. He had seen many women and had given thirtham and prasadam into many hands. But he had never trembled like this. He saw her place the flowers he had given her in her hair and the sandalwood paste on her forehead. Then she turned and went away. Others took her place. He poured holy water into their hands with a sense of detachment.

From the next day onward, people felt that the image had become holier. It was decorated beautifully. In the red hue of the sandalwood paste covering it, the face seemed touched with the tender promise of a smile. A deep loveliness glowed in the corners of her kohl-rimmed eyes. Her red silk garment with its fine golden fringe shone brightly in the radiance of the lamps. It was impossible for anyone to stand at that shrine and not join their hands in worship.

The young woman came every day at dusk. He gave her some prasadam. He noticed with astonishment that she held a wedding garland of fresh champakam flowers exactly like the one in the hands of the Devi.

The temple was well known for fulfilling the prayers of unmarried girls and granting them the boon of marriage. None of the girls who had prayed and made offerings there had gone away disappointed. Mothers took comfort from the temple, and lovers who desired each other offered everything they had in the hope of being united. Young men and women came from distant places to pray there. And so the sweet longings, the desires, and the appeals of many human lives blossomed in front of the Devi.

Only the priest was not granted this blessing, for he who performed the daily worship of the maiden goddess had to remain unmarried. He could not talk to or live with a woman, not even his mother. He was not permitted to think about anything in this world except the Devi. That was the rule.

The young devotee had never regretted this or grieved over the vow he had made. He had been born into a family that could proudly claim Sri Sankara[1] as an ancestor. His blood throbbed when he thought of this personification of knowledge and renunciation. The world had never seen such deep detachment, such astonishing intelligence, such great achievement, after his time. Why could not he, the priest, carry on the tradition? He knew that if he wanted to learn the truth of the world, he had to stand away from it. So as a first step he had accepted the position of a priest in the Devi temple. He had heard that the divine teacher had worked here to acquire *siddhi* or supreme knowledge.

The position carried a salary that anyone would have found attractive. But he did not accept it. If money was what he had wanted, the family he had left behind was very wealthy. Even princesses had tried to ensnare him and had named the price they would pay. But the sense of right and wrong that he had inherited from his forefathers protected him. And he knew he could raise himself by becoming the heir to immortal wealth.

Five years. He had spent five long years in constant worship and meditation of the image of the Devi. The shadows of the outside world had not been able to destroy the solitude of his soul. And yet, today, in the pure light of dusk, why had the beautiful young face so like the Devi's come into his range of vision? Had he slipped from the soul's immeasurable beauty to the glitter of the outside world? His heart trembled with the fear of having committed a sin. Ambike![2] Had he done wrong? What had been gained through the untiring effort of many births could be shattered, he knew, by a moment's weakness.

After that he never looked at the young woman's face. And yet, as he placed the sacred water and offerings respectfully, expressionlessly, in the many hands stretched out to him, he trembled when he saw a hand like a reddish petal.

The priest lived in a small house adjoining the temple garden. When the noon and night rituals and prayers were over, he studied the marvellous teachings of the great Puranic sages and thought of new ways to interpret them. He wondered whether these new interpretations had already been found. The deeper one went into the great sea of knowledge, the more profound it became. He was fully submerged by its waves.

Flowers bloomed around the house. The moon often wandered through the sky, shedding a milky white smile. The scented breeze caressed the trees with a soft murmur. Whatever the season, the birds in the garden sang sweetly. But the priest knew nothing of all this. Nothing touched him.

He tried to work out the precise meanings of the complex Vedanta Sutras. *"Brahmam satyam jaganmithya,"* "The Supreme Being is the truth, the world is illusion." Why did people struggle so hard for something so transient? Time danced through an endless succession of moments. As we were born and as we died over and over again, we rose and fell like bubbles in the great sea of power. The smallest drop that wished to become a pearl in the limitless ocean had to free itself of all bonds. He thought he must somehow finish writing his book. Maybe it would grant peace to generations of people.

That day, as usual, he took out the great tome and opened it. But the letters on the worn, moth-eaten page refused to take shape in the light of the smoking oil lamp. For the first time in his life, his body thrilled to the cool summer breeze blowing in from outside. The waves of a sweet music that contained the whole world within it made him restless deep inside.

The young priest closed his book, feeling uneasy, and began to walk in the courtyard. The scent of a champakam tree, covered with golden flowers, intoxicated him. He had picked up an ax many times to cut it down because the tree seemed so unsuited to an ashram. But he had not been able to destroy this sweet gift of summer. He had not found the courage to do this, although he had nipped his own tender emotions as they blossomed. And so, he had always offered all its flowers to the virgin goddess.

Was love a crime? Was beauty contemptible? In that case, why did Mother Nature, who created the stars in the sky and the flowers of the earth, diffuse love and beauty? He recalled the musical verses of the Sama Veda. Did they not keep alive this great beauty? For whom did his own Devi, his favorite goddess, wait with an eternally fresh garland? He felt that it was not possible to deny the universal emotions of the heart. But could they not be elevated to the level of a divine, eternal experience?

A bird that had grown intoxicated on eating mango shoots, sang near him. Bees hummed, shaking awake midnight flowers. He wandered through this dreamlike nocturnal landscape singing the beautiful hymns written by the great religious teachers.

Time passed. The same things happened over and over again. But one day she did not come. The scented sticks burned out and had to be lit again. The thirtham water in the kindi filled up repeatedly like the water of the Ganga. Darkness covered the night, and yet she did not come. That day, or the next, or for many days.

The image of the virgin goddess glowed with the sad smile of one distressed by the pain of separation. He continued his worship with ceaseless and attentive devotion. The reputation of the temple grew. People were certain that whatever they prayed for would be granted. No other temple had such a divine priest. He was considered a god. Innumerable devotees poured in every day. He gave them all his blessing. But he was never blessed in return.

The trees that had flowered bore fruit. Pigeons laid eggs in the rafters of the small house. He did not want to drive them away. Cows wandered inside the temple walls, their udders full. Mother Nature enchanted him.

It was a new moon night. There was a clear crescent moon in the sky. The bright glow of sunset dissolved into the white moonlight. He opened the door of the sanctum as usual, a platter blazing with fire in his hand. Amazing! Even the rays of light were transfixed for a moment. She was there, the lovely young woman who looked so like the Devi!

She held a fresh champakam bud to her high breasts, a little blossom that had taken shape from her own champakam-like body. She laid it as an offering at the Devi's holy feet with pride. What can a woman offer God with as much satisfaction as her own child?

The little one stretched out its hands and sprang toward the door, its smile dripping honey. The priest thought that a baby's unclear lisp was more powerful than the chanting of mantrams. It seemed to him that the Devi herself came forward to gather the infant to her breast.

The priest gazed steadily at the child, wanting to give it a kiss. But that would be shameful. So many children came to the temple. Why should this one be special? He took a handful of *trimadhuram* from the foot of the image and threw it into the baby's hands. The child handed it back smilingly. He did not take it. Laughing delightedly, the child thrust the nectar in its hands into his mother's mouth.

The priest looked on and blessed them with a feeling of perfect fulfillment. They blessed him as well. When she kissed the little golden flower and turned away, he felt as if the radiant lamps around him had grown dim. After that, he always gave trimadhuram to all the children who came to the temple.

However hungry he was, he used to go up first to the attic in his house to scatter rice and paddy for the baby pigeons while their parents were out looking for food. He gave all the bananas and *payasam* left over from the offerings to the frolicking calves. Sometimes, he gave them his own food and took pleasure in observing a fast.

The temple began to acquire a reputation not only for granting the boon of marriage to unmarried girls, but also for making childless women conceive. Many barren women who came there scattered rice for the pigeons and fed the calves. Those who came empty were fulfilled. The wheels of time continued to turn. Many trees in the garden dried up, some fell and broke. New ones had to be planted. The little baby birds became full-grown pigeons and laid eggs in their turn. The eggs hatched, became pigeons, and flew away. But there were always pigeons in the eaves of the small house. And flowers in the garden. And the same priest offered them to the image of the Devi.

The white clouds of summer filled the sky. The tired evening breeze blew over nature's parched body. The solitary evening star rose with a pure light that diffused sorrow. Sandhya, the Goddess of Dusk, wiped away her vermilion mark and searched for her star chains to say her prayers. The conch sounded from the Devi temple for the evening worship. It took no note of the passage of time. The temple bells, accompanied by the chanting of mantrams, echoed with a grandeur that seemed not of this world. There was always something fresh and new in its sound. The crowd at the temple door grew. The doors of heaven would open now.

The priest appeared, looking like a god who granted boons. His platter, radiant with light, dispelled the darkness outside. His eyes were filled with an incredibly peaceful message of benediction. He looked around him.

A woman's form came out of the crowd. Her hair was as white as her clothes. Her forehead was covered with holy ash. Her trembling fingers counted the moments of time on her *japamala*. She joined her palms. He could not help doing so as well, for her greeting was full of dignity and she had the look of one who had attained perfect fulfillment. She laid her tulasi chain, untouched by the slightest trace of desire, at the door. He looked at the image, and at her. Astonishing! His eyes lowered themselves unconsciously.

After many days, by the light of the holy flames he saw his face clearly in the sacred water he held in his hands. It was not the expressionless face of a yogi who had renounced the world. It was the face of a worldly man, a lover. He realized that what he had worshipped all these days was not the image of the Devi, but its completely human and worldly reflection in the flesh. The emotions he had suppressed in the dormant inner recesses of his being had taken a new shape. And so, before that stone image, he had unknowingly obeyed, experienced, and manifested a human consciousness and allowed it to grow. He had run away from life, calling all truth an illusion. But that life had had to contain him within it for its own fulfillment.

He recalled everything that had happened from the day he had first seen the woman. As far as he was concerned, she had been a symbol of the outside world. Had he not been attracted to her, he would have hated all living things. A human being can attain the experience of the eternal and the divine only through another human being. He raised his head. The flowers on the pedestal of the image had begun to fade. In the dim light of the lamps, the image had a look of dark seriousness. The flames in the big platter smoked and burned low. An intense darkness filled the entire world.

The woman had worshipped and left. Everyone had left. The priest stared at the image as if the veil hiding a great secret had been moved from his eyes.

"Deceptive, illusory seductress! Cruel woman! You have finally shown me your true form. You will not be able to trick me anymore. Your floral offerings from yesterday's worship that I have to throw away today, were the petals of my beautiful dreams. What you allowed to burn out and die were the tender shoots of my life's ideals. I offered everything I had at the feet of your stone image. I can renounce only that which I have achieved. And, great renouncer that I am, in this darkness I surrender you, which is all I have of my own, and go out into the limitlessness of freedom, into the great temple of the world. There, I can become a god myself."

He took off all the jewels that adorned the image, burned them, and threw them in front of the image. In the ghastly light of the blazing flames, the image seemed to him as fearful as the form of Kali, the Devi in her avenging form.

The next day, people saw the priest sitting on the roadside, wiping a child's tears. It was rumored that he had been expelled for having taken out all the money from the treasury, distributing it to the poor.

1943

NOTES

1. Ninth-century namboodiri philosopher, credited with endowing Hinduism with a philosophical dimension. He established the doctrine of Advaita.
2. One of the names of the Devi.

Life and Death

H E HAD BEEN ill and confined to bed for two years before he died. He survived all of six months after the doctors had given up hope. Even his parents had prayed that death would release him from his suffering. And yet, the young widow fell at the feet of the corpse, struck her palms against her head, and wept bitterly. She took off her jewels and flung them away. Crazed with grief, she beat her breasts with her fists. No one tried to prevent her. No one dared console her. What comfort could anyone offer her, after all?

Both had been so full of hope when they got married. Before the first year was over—a short one that flashed by with the swiftness of lightning, aglow in the radiance of their honeymoon—he had become a sick man and she his nurse. She had battled for days with fear and hope in turn. Enormous sums of money had been spent on his treatment. No victim of tuberculosis had ever been nursed with such devotion.

And now it was all over. The dead go away. But what of her? She felt dead, but was still alive. She was only nineteen. How many long, empty days and nights, months and years, must creep by before her body could die and be laid on a funeral pyre. What harrowing ordeals she would have to face. Even her grim, stern father-in-law broke down and wept.

During the period of mourning, she immersed herself in the tank thrice a day, as custom demanded, and lay down dripping wet. She lived for ten whole days on mere mouthfuls of tender coconut water. Not by a fraction of an inch did she swerve from the rules prescribed for a widow. Relatives tried to dissuade her, talk her out of her rigid adherence to ritual. Customs were not all that strict anymore, they said. Even the senior woman of the household tried to reason with her. But Tatri[1] was adamant. She was determined to do everything that might be necessary to ensure the repose of her husband's soul. She knew she would not be satisfied until she had made every sacrifice she possibly could.

If she had had a son, he would have observed the mourning rituals over a year, but she did not have one. Instead, she performed all the funeral rites herself, paying scrupulous attention to every detail. Had her husband lived, she might have had a son. It seemed to her that she held this son within her body. She refused new clothes, would wear only a *mundu* that came up to her knees. She did not apply oil on herself when she had a bath, and ate a bare handful of rice once a day. She observed a whole year's mourning in this manner. The old and the orthodox were amazed. "Tatri is too severe with herself," they said. "Who would have imagined that she would be so unrelenting."

Although her parents-in-law sympathized with her for the hardships she imposed upon herself, deep in their hearts they were also pleased that she showed her husband—and their son—such devotion. No one had really expected it of her, for she was not a child of the old world. The young man had married her for her education and her modern views, and not for money. And he had done so without his parents' consent. Since he was an ardent supporter of social reform, his parents had dreaded that he would involve his wife in his activities. But nothing of the sort had happened. There had been no time, destiny had willed otherwise.

Tatri was seated in the kitchen on her husband's first death anniversary, her throat dry and parched after the year's interminable rites. She drew a sigh of relief. She had done everything possible for her husband's body and soul. Being a childless widow, she now had no more duties to fulfill in the world. But life had to go on, a life burning itself out in its nonexistence.

Throughout the year, she had seemed utterly oblivious of herself. Death had dominated her thoughts. It seemed as if while she performed the rites for her dead husband the dreadful stillness of his final moments had seeped into her. Dead inside, she had continued to live. Something had forced her to carry out her everyday tasks mechanically. She felt that the living being who had performed the rituals of mourning for the peace of the dead soul was no longer alive, but dead.

That night, when she exchanged the rough black blanket that she had used during the period of mourning for an ordinary sheet, her husband's form surfaced in her memory for the first time in months. She had not thought of him like this for a long time now. All she had been able to visualize was a nebulous shadow of death, a wrinkled, shriveled face, eyes that protruded from their sockets, and an incessant cough that spattered blood. And the awful stillness of the face at the moment of death. This image was not that of her beloved husband, the handsome young man whose tender touch had awakened her emotions that enchanted night.

They had met a year and a half before they were married. She had been a young schoolgirl. He had been invited to speak at the annual function at her school. She had heard of him, of course. He was known to be a radical social reformer, a man who scattered seeds of fire wherever he went. A short play that he had written, which had affected even moderate thinkers deeply, was being performed that evening. It revolved around a young widow caught in the steely clutches of tradition. Under the influence of changing social mores, she seeks a new life with her lover. Most of the girls at school had been reluctant to play the role of a widow, even on stage. Fifteen-year-old Savitri had come forward enthusiastically. "If no one else will do the part, I will," she said. "Why cancel the performance because no one wants to play the part of a widow? Tell the cowards to go away, and to sing the songs and dance the Mangalayathira that promise them long married lives."

It was a courageous thing to have done. Pretty and glowing, she had eyes that seemed naturally moist. When she came on stage with her disheveled hair, a *rudraksha* chain around her neck and *vibhuti* smeared on her forehead, looking the very incarnation of sorrow, the entire audience was moved to tears. Even the most conservative among them, who were sworn enemies of widow remarriage, conceded that it could be permitted under exceptional circumstances. The moderates were, of course, unanimous in their approval. The playwright was congratulated. A young man was inspired to get up and announce that he was prepared to accept a widow who was willing to remarry as his wife. The play was an unqualified success.

Meanwhile, the young playwright had been observing the actress who had played the heroine's role. He had attempted to assess her performance with critical concentration, with the impartiality of a reviewer. When the play was over and the cries of congratulations and the warm manifestations of approval had died down, he went up to the stage with a fast-beating heart. He took off the expensive watch he wore, placed it on the table, and said, "I present the praise showered on me and the encouragement it has given society to effect changes, together with this watch, to the young girl who played the heroine."

The spectators applauded. As the girl took the gift shyly, her head bent, the watch fell from her trembling hands, and its glass shattered into fragments. It seemed a terrible omen. There was a flutter even amongst the least superstitious in the audience.

He married her a year and a half later, braving opposition from his friends and relatives, paying no attention to the fact that she was not as rich as he was, or as aristocratic. He declared to her that along with the watch that ticked the seconds of time, he had also given her a heart that throbbed with love. Tatri shivered, recalling these incidents. His first gift to her, the gift that he had thought would last for all time, had been shattered. The hands and heart that gave it, and those that had received it, were blighted too. Was it for this that she had dressed up in widow's clothes and won accolades? Her husband had had the same thought in his last days, and, as disease changed him, he had given up his progressive views for older ideals. Once, he had said to her, "Tatrikutty,[2] you should never have played the role. The very first time I saw you,

you were dressed as a widow, and that image of yours is going to become real now."

There was a strong element of superstition underlying his reproach. She was tempted to retort, "Wasn't it because you wrote the play that I acted in it?" But she said nothing. Tatri had grown very quiet, she was no longer the argumentative girl she had once been.

Lying in bed, he would often touch her chains and bangles. What if they had to be taken off her lovely limbs? She sometimes felt that that was what he wanted. Once, for no reason at all, he rubbed the *thilakam* off her forehead. She never demurred, no matter what he said or did. She cared for him devotedly, enduring everything, never uttering an unworthy word, never distressing him with tears or sighs. But now, all the tears that she had held in check flowed unrestrainedly, an unceasing torrent.

She tried her hardest to turn her mind to other things. Once her kitchen work and worship were over, she spent her time reading. She first read the Puranams, then poems, plays, and novels. She turned from the path of devotion, through those of knowledge and action, into a variety of subjects. She had not read so much even when she was a student. Was it for her that her husband had bought so many books?

Her body grew healthier with a more normal routine, and her heart became calmer. She began to smile occasionally at her old companions. She dressed with more care. On moonlit nights, she stood at the window and hummed under her breath, sad little tunes that were the first tentative expressions of a heart that had been silent too long.

Her parents-in-law showed no displeasure toward their unfortunate daughter-in-law. But when the question of her husband's younger brother's marriage arose, his mother cautioned him, "Kuttan, make sure the horoscopes are well matched. If Chovva[3] or a gulikan[4] is in the eighth lunar position . . . We have had a bad experience, that's why . . ."

Tatri heard from behind the door and shuddered. She remembered that there had been complaints about her horoscope, but no one had paid attention. No one had cared to find out what exactly was wrong. For her husband had argued that it was hearts that had to match, and not horoscopes. And the result?

She thought unhappily about it all day.

Her brother-in-law married a girl from an established family, who carried with her a handsome dowry. When she was brought home, her mother-in-law counseled her in Tatri's hearing, "Hold your black thread tight, child, and pray.[5] Learning English won't do you any good. What is important is that your husband lives long."

Tatri had never held her black thread and prayed. She had worn a gold chain.

The younger brother began to visit the *antahpuram* often, now that he was married. He was pleasant and good-looking. He had been a student at the time of her marriage. She had seen him with his brother sometimes and found him a gentle, lovable child. Although she had seen him many times since, it was only now that she noticed the astonishing resemblance he had to her husband. Those shining eyes under the thick eyebrows, that broad forehead, that squarish, light-skinned face . . . He was three years younger than his brother, and at the same age now as her husband had been when he died. When he called out in a voice that seemed to her beautifully suited for chanting the Vedas, she longed to respond. Was everything that had happened to her only a dream? Startled into reality, Savitri shivered and ran away. She did not eat or sleep that day. Her consciousness slithered on the edge of a great precipice.

She was only six months older than the bride, and four years younger than her brother-in-law. If the older brother had not married her, she would have still been a virgin. So what? She hated the honey bee that hovered around her, but it would not go away. It stung her, over and over again, hurting her viciously. Enmeshed in her sinful thoughts, she finally fell into a black well of unconsciousness.

It was the night the bride and bridegroom were to be together for the first time. The usual preparations were on: there were perfumes, flower garlands, the intoxicating sounds of ululation. Married women were adorning the bride. The house was full of noise and laughter. Savitri lay prone in bed, hugging herself. She had not slept for the last three nights. She had a fever. But no one had time to spare for a widow in the midst of the festivities. Her fevered brain ached as she lay isolated from the bustle and grappled with her painful thoughts. They must be enjoying themselves now in that room. Everyone was so happy. Why couldn't she be happy too? How long would she have to live, incarcerated in this cell of darkness, benumbed, and alone, with only memories for company? She looked back on her life in the light of the ideals she had learned and believed in. To sacrifice life for one's belief in death— was this a sin or a virtue? Emotions she had wanted to forget over many days, which she had almost succeeded in forgetting, touched her heart again. The last scene of the play which her husband had written and she had acted in surfaced clearly in her mind.

"Evil spirits! Get away from me, I am being born anew into a life of which I can be proud, into the radiance of hope, into the bridal chamber of bliss—"

The words danced and swayed around her.

At midnight, there was a knock at the bridegroom's door. They told him that Tatri was ill, that they had found her screaming and thrashing her limbs in a frenzy. Her eyes protruded from their sockets, her lips were twisted, and she looked like one possessed. The whole household woke up. The *vaidyan* was summoned, and so was the sorcerer. The doctor followed on their heels.

The sorcerer pronounced his verdict—she was possessed by her husband's spirit. The vaidyan was certain that her raging fever was to blame for her condition. After a thorough examination, the doctor asked her brother-in-law, "Is she married?" He shook his head sadly and answered, "She is a widow. Our society does not permit widows to remarry."

"Is that so? Then—" The doctor thought for a long, long time. Then he said, "In that case, you and your society will have to learn to live with her incurable hysteria."

She was still screaming, "You demons! Go away!"

1946

NOTES

1. Short form of Savitri.
2. *Kutty* means "child", and may be used as a term of endearment by any older person for someone younger.
3. The planet Mars; if this planet is not well-positioned in a horoscope, the marriage will not be happy.
4. A demon or a star that brings forth misfortune.
5. Married women are supposed to hold the mangalyasutram or thread, which they wear round their necks, in their hands while chanting mantrams, since that ensures long-lasting wedded bliss.

A Leaf in the Whirlwind

KODUMKATTILPETTA ORILA 9

S HE WAS THE most emaciated of the women in the group, and the most agitated as well. An agreement had been made to hand over fifty women who had been held captive this side of the border,[1] in return for an equal number from the other side. She was part of this group, and was from a village in western Punjab. The exchange was effected at the frontier. Bundled shapelessly in black, the women glided from one side to the other like ghosts released from a tomb. She was the last to go through, refusing to give her name or her caste, even seeming reluctant to go to the refugee camp. She held back and asked, "Are you taking us from one prison to another, then?"

The vehicles were ready with an escort of army and police personnel. The members of the sevak sangham[2] spoke generous words of comfort and encouragement to the women. She resisted still, and had to be forced to step into the vehicle.

Although there was an acute lack of space in the refugee camp, the women were given greater facilities than they had hoped for. They were regarded as children returned from the dead. Some of them had relatives in the area, others were in search of their families. She alone would not talk to anyone. She sat in a corner by herself, her head bent, and refused to remove her purdah. When a sevika[3] brought her food, she shouted, "Throw away your rotten pieces of bread. Give me a gun, or a dagger—or even some poison. That's all I want from you."

They did not know what to do. The woman must be mad, they thought. Not surprising, though. It was a wonder that these women were alive at all, after the horror and the trauma that they had endured. Many of them wept incessantly. Some told each other their terrible stories. There was an old woman who had had nine children and fifty grandchildren, and who had been like a mother to her entire village. She had given food and shelter to Hindu and Muslim refugees alike. Her family had refused to move, even when they were warned that danger was imminent, because of her obstinate desire to die on the soil on which she had been born. All the children were dead now. The girls had been raped. The old woman had stood in the courtyard of her beloved home and watched it burn and turn to ashes. Yet, she was still alive. She cried constantly, even when she ate or slept, but continued to talk, greedy for a part in life.

A young woman painfully chewed the dry morsels of chappati they had been given for breakfast. Her cheeks and chest were swollen and her clothes tattered. The wife of a rich businessman in Sind, she had set out with her three children as soon as she heard that trouble was expected. But disaster had moved faster than her car and caught up with her. Her husband was killed and she was raped beside his lacerated body by men whose hands were stained with her children's blood. She had been barely alive when she was picked up from a railway track—yet she had not died.

A young Sikh girl consoled a Hindu child. An infant cried itself to sleep. Little ones wailed for parents who had disappeared. Many women had run long distances in their desperate bid to escape the killers and had feet that were badly sore and wounded. Some had maimed bodies. Fever and infections were common. The inmates of the camp, however, were learning to accept these lesser misfortunes as a part of their lives.

The young woman observed everything. She did not weep, but a despair more profound than tears filled her eyes. Sometimes she looked as if she hated the world. It was four days now since she had eaten, but her stomach still bulged out, and she stared at it constantly, knotting her fists tightly.

The people in the camp were attracted to her. Small, delicate, and beautiful, she was like a tender crescent moon. She seemed to come from an aristocratic family, to have been once a cherished daughter and wife, who had known nothing but happiness. It did not look as if she could be allowed to starve herself much longer, and since she still refused to eat, a doctor was called in to see her.

The doctor tried his best to coax her to drink some milk. "Please, Sister, drink this—if not for your own sake, at least for ours. Our beloved country values every life it has."

"Every life, indeed," she burst out. "This despicable country has already destroyed so many thousands of lives. Maybe I am despicable too. But why should I continue to live, if it is only to sow the seeds of destruction?" She sobbed and went on. "Let me ask you something, Doctor. Will you destroy what you wish to destroy in the same way that you save what you wish to save? Do you believe that you can save a life by destroying the fruit of animal force and ignorance?" She looked anxiously at him, her eyebrows raised. His face grew pale. Her question made him uneasy. He was a disciple of the great Indian teacher of ahimsa, on whose suggestion he had given up a secure and well-paid position and come here. He knew what she meant, and he had an answer. His instruments were at hand. But would it be right to do what she asked of him? A great fear took hold of him. He knew that whether he broke an egg, or strangled someone's neck, it would end a life—these were merely different ways of killing.

He told her, with the air of a mature philosopher, "Sister! We cannot fight against the irrevocable dictates of fate. As a doctor, I have the right only to save, not to destroy. Look at the hundreds of thousands of people in this camp. There are many more camps like this. A terrible whirlwind blows through our unfortunate motherland now from all directions. But Bharat is sure to survive, and you are a woman of Bharat, aren't you? Come now, drink this milk—"

She made no reply to this long sermon, but she drank the milk. Either the doctor's words had moved her, or she had reached the limits of despair and now wanted to live. She began to eat regularly as well.

Her name had been put down in the camp register as Jyoti. A Sikh woman who came from her village said that her full name was Jyotirmayi Devpal. She described how Jyoti had refused to accept purdah as she grew up and of how she had rejected a proposal of marriage from a zamindar. The village women had been shocked at her behavior. Maybe she was being punished now for her impudence.

The crowds in the refugee camp increased steadily. They were dressed in different ways and spoke various languages. There were men, women, and children who ranged from the very young to the very old. As their numbers grew, there were more stories to talk about, more noise and confusion. No one was particularly interested in Jyoti anymore. She merged like a wave into the great flood of people. She witnessed innumerable births and deaths, and many incidents that were a part of living.

Every evening, when the sun sank below the western horizon, people gathered under the tamala tree in the camp. Many of them were villagers and did not understand national problems. These beloved children of a land where five great rivers and sweet meadows filled the earth with prosperity, still dreamed of the buffaloes that grazed there, the swaying wheat fields that laughed in the wind, the herds of camels that moved slowly through the villages. They remembered walking home on so many evenings like these, with their tools on their shoulders, humming to themselves, to the houses that had been theirs through many generations, and which their children would inherit. But they had been driven out of their homes like stray dogs, and hunted like wildfowl. Why? Whose fault was it?

The refugees often cursed the famous leaders of the nation and ground their teeth, longing for revenge. Some even grumbled at the "toothless old man"[4] who was said to be such a saintly person. Poor things, they had suffered deeply, but had never inflicted suffering on others. Did the people in the camps across the border feel the same way?

Jyoti listened to what everyone said, but kept to herself, trying to hide her swollen stomach in the folds of her saree. She wanted as few people as possible to know her secret—that she was an unmarried pregnant woman who was at present being sheltered by society. Her burden became heavier as the days went by. The vague tremors that curled through her like little waves grew into a suffocating flood of movements that invaded every atom of her body, proclaiming their victorious power over her. They were the image of a contemptible aspect of the human spirit, of people who despised womanhood, humanity, and a belief in the goodness of things. The image was growing within her now, it was part of her lifeblood, her very breath. One day her shame would manifest its cosmic form, regardless of whether she, or anyone else, wanted it to do so. There was no way out.

She lay prone, her stomach pressed to the ground, enduring it all. There was nothing else that she could do.

An extraordinary thing happened one day. A newborn baby's body was found in the camp latrine. A beautiful plump baby, as sleek as a clot of blood. It was as light-skinned as the border people and its hair was copper colored. There was a bluish crescent shaped mark on its neck. The scavengers carried away its body, which was still warm. None of the women wept and no one was accused.

Jyoti bit into her lips as she watched. She realized that these women were remarkably courageous and practical, although they were often called cowards and slaves. They did not hesitate, once they made up their minds, nor did they waver. They did not ask anyone for advice. They overcame whatever obstacles they encountered and headed toward their goal. Jyoti's heart beat faster than the quickenings in her stomach. It was such an easy thing to do, of such little consequence. It obviously took less time than it took to pluck a blade of grass—half a second, perhaps, or a minute at the most. She could wipe away the stain in the darkness of the night and come out into a new world full of hope.

She wandered over the deserted areas outside the camp all day and crept into a lonely corner to sleep at night. One day, while she ate, her back began to hurt badly and her head started to spin. She felt frightened. What could it be? Was this a precursor of the great event? Ayyo! Then—

Nothing happened, however, and no one suspected anything. Fainting spells were common in the camp. Weeks went by.

An important and well-known visitor came to the camp. He had been sent with a message from the Mahatma. He spoke to the people gathered under the tamala tree and told them that young men must be prepared to accept the victims of rape as their mothers, their sisters, or even as their wives. Jyoti listened attentively as he went on, "The children they bear are the citizens of Bharat— the new citizens of a free Bharat."

Jyoti's face turned the color of flaming coal. What a contradiction this was! How could such children be the citizens of Bharat alone, of Bharat as it was today? They would grow up and their tender minds would begin to grasp the truth. They would learn that the blood in their veins had spurted from hate and not from love. Would not a fierce desire for revenge take hold of them, then, and would they not shatter the country's frontiers to achieve their revenge?

When she awoke from her fearful imaginings about the future, she was alone. The visitor must have left. Everyone else had left as well. The night had grown very dark and cold. She got up to go back to the camp and found that she could not move. Her body trembled and she felt helpless. A sharp pain raced through her body with the rapidity of lightning. Was this the pain of creation? She held onto one of the lower branches of the tamala tree and tried to endure the agony.

She was not sure how long she stood there. Indistinct memories surfaced in her mind. She thought of a wealthy household in a prosperous village in distant Punjab. A woman lay in great pain, surrounded by doctors and nurses. Her relatives and friends were anxious about her, and her husband kept watching the hands of the clock move. All of them were impatient to know the result of the long treatment that the woman had undergone and the innumerable rituals that had been performed so that she could have a child.

She gave birth to a baby girl. Her entire family and the whole village cherished the happy little child. No one ever said anything unkind to her. When she grew up, her parents were reluctant to send her to college, but she charmed them into letting her go. Her family was distressed when she abandoned purdah, but they did not protest. She spurned an offer of marriage because she wanted to remain free. She never thought of freedom as her exclusive right, but longed to shatter the chains of slavery that bound her society and her country and liberate the whole oppressed multitude of humanity. She wanted to give them the will power to act for themselves. She was obsessed with the desire to unite all people and all things in a web of love.

Beautiful, wealthy, and cherished as she was, she joined the nationalist movement, went to jail, and worked tirelessly, without regular food or sleep. She was warned when trouble was expected, but she continued with her work for the poor and the weak. Her constant slogan was, "I trust my brothers!" And the result—

"Amme!" She was forced to the ground by repeated stabs of pain. Her body was drenched in sweat and nausea choked her. Exhausted, she got up again and leaned against the tamala tree.

Frightening memories crowded into her mind.

Fifteen women, who were in purdah, hid in her neighbor's house. The master of the household, Kassim, was a close friend of her father, and his daughter, Ayesha, had been a beloved companion for years. Ayesha had arranged to shelter them in her house in spite of her brother Ali, who always insisted, "Gold will not sprout in our soil unless it is soaked in the blood of *kafirs*!"

Ayesha took great care to make sure that her brother did not suspect anything. Her father's cart went regularly to town with bales of straw. There was a refugee camp just beyond the border. Kassim Saheb's cart had gone that way for fifty years. They were sure that no one would bar its way.

Jyoti thought of that terrible journey. In the suffocating darkness of the wire cage they could hear the shouts of slogans and the wails of victims. They smelt burning flesh and felt the heat of flames. Kassim Saheb cried out, *"Pakistan zindabad! Allah ho Akbar!"* "Long live Pakistan, Allah is great!" as if he believed it would save them. They began to think that the danger was past. There was a sudden commotion, and the cart stopped. Kassim Saheb's oaths and protests were ignored, and the bales of straw were pulled out. There was raucous laughter, followed by agonized cries. Fifteen young girls, fragile and innocent, were seized and thrown cruelly one by one to the ground.

Ayyo! She felt that her pain would suffocate her. Was this the agony of birth or of death? It seemed to her that her mother came up to her and said, "I endured this too, Jyoti, and so did my mother and her mother before her. All mothers must endure this pain." She had to pay the price for being a woman.

She remembered the prison where she had lain unconscious. Innumerable men had entered that room. She thought of their faces, maddened with communal fever, flushed with hate, devilish. Which of them would her baby look like?

She shivered. She was hot and thirsty. Every breath she took was a throb of pain.

Ah—it was over at last. Was it really over?

The lights had come on in the sheds in the camp. The sick groaned. Children screamed. Clearly, no one knew what had happened to her.

She lay stretched out on the grass, like a triumphant hero who has collapsed on the battlefield. The stars had grown dim. A baby bird in the tamala tree beat its wings and chirped. What was she to do?

She could close her eyes tight, grope in the darkness, find it, and crush it to death. She could then bury the pain and humiliation of all these days under the trees, along with its body. She did not want a scavenger to drag it along the ground and dispose of it. This was her cross, she had borne it, and she had to lay it down herself.

The owls hooted impatiently—it's time, it's time. She got up slowly, stretched out her hand, and touched the mass of moving flesh. How hot its body felt, it burned her. Had it taken this heat from her own body? Perhaps it looked like her as well. What if she opened those tender eyes and looked into them? She longed to look, just once.

"Hna . . . a . . ."

It tossed its arms and legs and seemed to ask for protection. Its voice was not like hers. It was not like any voice she knew, or that she had heard before. The voice rose steadily, a primeval human demand on nature—"Hna . . . a . . ."

She thought the sound would wake everyone in the camp. It seemed as if the whole world, everything animate and inanimate, birds, beasts, even the unmoving earth, would merge with that cry and awaken. For it was so powerful. And so soft.

She put her hand over the parted lips to hush the sound. They had the ticklish softness of a leaf. She realized that what she felt was fear, not love. Someone seemed to be beside her, someone who commanded her not to restrain that cry, who told her that it was not the cry of a baby, but of the universe itself.

Jyoti drew back, startled. She was not sure what to do. She wanted to escape from the contradictory emotions she felt, and was full of fear and doubt. If only she could hide somewhere, beyond the edges of the earth, the underworld. Would this cry pursue her even there?

She wondered whether to let the child lie there, on the grass. She had heard that the gods always cared for a child abandoned by its mother. Someone would find it in the morning—some mother, perhaps, who did not have children. It suddenly struck her that she had a child now, a child of her own.

She felt confused, as if she had bitten on something both bitter and sweet. No, she thought, it was not possible to reject a bond that was so inextricably woven with her life, even if it brought her great sorrow. If she refused, she would inflict a permanent wound on herself, a wound that would fester and sting and hurt all her life. Jyoti went slowly toward the child. Although it was still crying, its voice was less steady now, and its limbs seemed much weaker. If she waited longer, there would be no need to make a decision.

The young mother gathered her son in her arms and hugged him. She kissed his icy forehead over and over again till it became warm. Her lifeblood flowed to the child as milk.

The mother walked toward the camp holding her little one to her breast. The stars smiled down on her as if they had found the answer to a difficult question.

1948

NOTES

1. The story is set in riot-torn Punjab during the partition of India in 1947, when Punjab and Bengal were divided between India and Pakistan.
2. Groups of volunteers formed to help the riot victims.
3. Female volunteer.
4. Referred to as the Mahatma later in the story, Mohandas Karamchand Gandhi (1869–1948), Indian nationalist leader who led the nation to independence through the path of ahimsa. Although venerated as a saint and immensely popular, Gandhi was also criticized for not being able to keep his vow that the partition would never be allowed, which explains the anger in the jibe "toothless old man."

"Come Back"

"THIRIKE VARU"

10

WHENEVER I THINK about women's associations, Bhanumathi Amma[1] comes to mind. Not that it is important in any way. I just think of her, that's all. I've called a number of young social workers Bhanumathi Amma by mistake, and then corrected myself. How forgetful I am! Why is that name hidden in my consciousness? Young girls today know very little about Bhanumathi Amma. I wonder what they would think of her?

There have been no women in our part of the country whose names posterity found it worthwhile to cherish. And even if there were, no one would ever have heard of them. A young poet once teased me, "Here they come, the great ones, claiming descent from the Rani of Jhansi and Padmini Devi! Tell me, is there a single Malayali woman who has distinguished herself for her contribution to art or literature, or social service, or even music?"

I was furious. I said, "There were mothers who bore children who did these things. Isn't that enough?"

This retort may have been made purely in self-defense, or in utter helplessness—for I had no answer. Anyway, I didn't bother to invent a list of names that one could conceivably be proud of. Or condemn. Bhanumathi Amma always said, "Our community will never progress unless women are willing to abandon old traditions

and notions of family prestige, until they are prepared to face whatever confronts them. They are choked and strangled, then laughed
at for not being able to sing or make speeches. The hands that
stifle them should be bitten, wrenched away, Chechi, even if it hurts
to do so."

She reminded me of Tennyson's princess. If women wished for
progress, they had to create a world that was exclusively theirs, in
which art, literature, sculpture, and education would have their special places. They would have to be taught the science of nationalism
and the conventions of political agitation. Ideally, they would have
to learn to live without being dependent on men. Bhanumathi
Amma would elaborate, "There will be no silks or perfumed oils,
no talcum powder, or cosmetics, not even a mirror, in that happy
land . . . We must do away with any emotion that makes us weak
or deceitful. If we can train five hundred women to live like this,
enrolling them when they are five, and keeping them till they're
twenty-five, victory will be ours. For they will take over—"

I found it difficult to agree entirely with Bhanumathi Amma's
ideals. But her integrity and dignity moved me. She perceived her
own future as part of the future of her community. Awake or asleep,
she brooded tirelessly: How could she ensure that women were
not laughed at, how could she help them overcome their foibles?
She believed firmly in self-fulfillment. She did not argue because
she thought it fashionable to do so, or because she had no logical
response, but because she was convinced about what she said.
Young, beautiful, well-educated, and aristocratic, she could have
chosen any career she wished. Or she could have married. Or
stayed at home and spent her days in idle chatter. Nothing com-
pelled her to wage this thankless war for social justice, to risk her
reputation, and endure hardships.

An inspired young woman like Bhanumathi could not contain
her ardor for long. All around her were innumerable companions,
whose natural talents were being stifled because they were trapped
in ignorance and slavery. They were little better, she thought, than
painted wooden dolls. Would she be able to touch them to life, to
inflame them? At least, she could give her life to them. She was
obsessed by all matters that concerned the self-esteem of women.

Her feelings gradually diffused themselves through her immediate surroundings and gave shape to a women's movement.

It began with a handful of women who formed a women's society and a library. They needed money for their activities, so they organized cultural programs and propaganda. Parents and guardians frowned at the thought of young girls of good families going out to beg for money, or dressing up to act on stage. But their wards broke away from their strict control. Revolutionary movements have their own unassailable force, after all. People were astonished —young girls who had been considered meek and gentle turned overnight into tiger cubs.

The women soon realized that they needed a meeting place for their activities and training programs. How long could they count on their parents' uncertain generosity? Nor did they want to rely on the kindness of strangers. Bhanumathi Amma rented a house in town—a quiet, clean, convenient place, with large grounds. It could house fifty people. Spinning and weaving sessions were started. Training classes and discussion groups were organized for the study of child care. Nothing had been systematically planned, but necessity being the mother of invention, one development led to another. People looked on, amazed. "What efficient women— they've managed to do in a day what took us a hundred years."

I remember with what resourcefulness and determination Bhanumathi Amma forged ahead. It seemed as if she felt that even a minute's hesitation might threaten her survival. Older women who had initially thought her crazy began to appreciate her integrity. Here was an establishment that women could respect, that made no distinctions of caste or creed, that took in rich and poor alike, whose simple lifestyle and ideals were easy to absorb. Women arrived from distant places. They obeyed Bhanumathi Amma with reverence, and tried to emulate her. Young girls were even willing to die for Bhanumathi Chechi.

This was the period when the waves of the freedom struggle were crashing throughout the country, and all associations were viewed with suspicion by the government. Bhanumathi Amma was not a nationalist. Indeed, she felt that nationalism had to be separated from social service. However, the wives and sisters of nationalist leaders who were in hiding, or in prison, were always welcome at the *sadanam*.[2] There was even a rumor that sometimes the leaders themselves came there stealthily. The secret police kept watch over the place night and day. "Excellent," said Bhanu, "our government is aware of its responsibilities. It would never do for a women's establishment to be left unguarded."

Astonishing as it was, it was precisely because of the government's natural suspicions and prohibitions that the sadanam grew so rapidly. The more the authorities opposed it, the closer people felt to it. Donations doubled, and so did the desire to cooperate. The workers were extremely enthusiastic. The precincts echoed to music and dance sessions. Loud flourishes of nationalist thought resounded from public platforms. Looms and spinning wheels whirred incessantly. Were our little girls, who had danced and sung, whimpered, and wept till yesterday, really capable of all this? People would point to Bhanumathi Amma—"That's the secretary of the sadanam. Aspiring social workers should learn from her example."

I thought that at least the annals of the next generation would include the name of a great Malayali woman.

Around this time, there was a proposal of marriage for Bhanumathi Amma from an unbelievably good quarter. Her family thought it an excellent match. She could not be a social worker forever. Moreover, marriage was the ideal foundation for a social worker to build on. In our country, a single woman lives a very restricted existence and has no access to many areas of social life. She does not even enjoy freedom of speech. She has to live constantly in an atmosphere of censure and suspicion. An unmarried social worker's reputation is like a soap bubble that could be blown away with a breath of air. A sneeze could shatter her future, and the future of the movement she participates in. Bhanumathi Amma's mother was aware of all this, and said to her, "Please say yes, child. Your associations and societies are not going to last forever. I can die in peace once I see you married."

Bhanumathi Amma shook her head. "No, Amme, it won't work. This is the way girls are coaxed into marriage. I won't ruin the country by not marrying. Let me find out if I can live honorably as an unmarried woman."

Her mother wept. Her father scolded. Relatives offered advice. But Bhanumathi Amma was adamant. She moved to her workplace. Her companions praised her courage. They kissed and cheered her. They swore they would endure anything, sacrifice anything, for Bhanumathi Chechi. Bhanumathi was so overcome, she burst into tears.

I've often wondered if Bhanu's act that day was really a sacrifice. Was it wise on her part? The greatest sacrifice one can make in the cause of duty is to renounce tenderness. And she had pulled tenderness out by its roots. Close observation revealed that Bhanumathi was very much like other women. She did not hate the world, nor was she harsh by nature. But when she prepared herself for action, she became detached, disciplined. The women's movement could not be limited to the *antahpuram*, after all. In order to shatter the concept of the antahpuram, women had to go out, meet men of different sorts and different ages. They had to oppose men, argue with them, sometimes plead with them for cooperation. They had to be cautious and crafty when they fought battles in such a dangerous area. Bhanumathi Amma therefore confronted the outside world with a judicious mixture of a schoolteacher's sternness and a *tarawad* matron's dignity. In pristine white khadar, wearing no make-up of any kind, the lovely young woman won the esteem of all who knew her.

But she was no sanyasini.

In matters concerning the discipline of the organization, Bhanumathi Amma took particular care to see that none of the girls played the coquette. She forbade them to speak about love or the softer emotions. The group observed the routine of a nunnery. I often wondered how soft, sensitive, poetic creatures like Radha survived there. Radha's entire life was beauty and poetry, poetry and beauty. Bhanumathi Amma often scolded her, as she flitted through kitchen, bathroom, and workroom, singing the love songs of Changampuzha.[3] And yet, Radha was Bhanumathi's closest friend. They were inseparable.

The intimacy between these two very different women was a source of great delight to me. Bhanumathi Amma was not a close friend of mine, but I knew many of her friends and met them often.

The women's movements of the period centered around her organization.

I think Bhanumathi Amma despised me, caught up as I was in family life, an old-fashioned woman with children and domestic worries. She thought that the greatest mistake a woman could make, the greatest curse that could befall her, was to give more importance to the bonds of family than to social relationships. Maybe she was right. I never argued the point with her. After all, I was such an insignificant person beside a dedicated, enthusiastic social worker like Bhanumathi Amma, a woman who considered no sacrifice too great for her to make.

It may have been the insistent demands of my family life that prevented me visiting the sadanam over a period of time. Radha's letters gave me bits and pieces of news. All public movements meet with a similar fate: after the first inspired phase, they grow sluggish, their heat and vigor abate. As long as their fundamental principles survive, they may not disintegrate. Nevertheless, the second phase, slow and tiresomely dull, is difficult to endure. There were quarrels. Old workers left, new ones joined. Because one particular party was well supported, others were offended. Radha wrote, "There are ugly rumors about Bhanumathi Chechi. What is worse, some of our workers believe them. Anyone except Bhanumathi Chechi would have left the place, shattered."

I could not accept Radha's words at face value, for she always magnified her smallest misgivings. But when I next met Bhanumathi Amma, she seemed to lack confidence. She told me they were shifting to a rural area in order to save money. They would then have more freedom too. Bhanumathi Amma fondled my child with unusual tenderness that day, something I had never seen her do before.

Time went by. I fell seriously ill and no longer knew what was happening in the outside world. Shapes moved around me like shadows, faint echoes of events reached me. Nothing was clear, nothing touched me. I was not surprised when I heard later that Bhanumathi Amma had gone away to a well-known women's ashram. A fine worker like her could not have been kept confined forever to a little place. I was certain that she was on her way to winning fame.

Many days passed. I met Radha unexpectedly on a train. She didn't recognize me at first. Maybe I would not have recognized her either, for she had grown very thin. There was no poetry in her eyes now, no smile on her lips. She no longer had the old vitality. She looked like a careworn housewife, settled into her existence. She looked up from the newspaper she was reading and gazed around aimlessly. Her eyes met mine. Doubt, recollection, and recognition succeeded each other. She sprang forward and hugged me, her laugh spilling delight. "Ayyo, my sister!"

Quite overcome, she laid her head on my shoulder like a child, her eyes full of tears. I could hear her heart beat very fast. "Oh, sister, you've changed so much, so very, very much. No one else but I would have recognized you—"

"I know," I said, my voice choked. "We've all changed, Radha! I, you, all of us. But so long as there's something within us that hasn't changed—"

Radha's story was an ordinary one. After the break up of the sadanam, she had returned home and got married. She had three children. She taught in a primary school. School work, childbearing, and running a home had all combined to crush her health and poetic gifts. And yet, she seemed happy enough. When we talked about the sadanam, Radha said, "I'm not unhappy. When I think of what happened to Bhanumathi Chechi—oh, that was so shameful—"

I was aghast. "What do you mean? I thought she was in an ashram somewhere. Did she join a revolutionary party or something like that?"

Radha looked hurt. "Revolutionary party, indeed! That would have been a good thing. But this! That Bhanu Chechi, who forbade us to laugh or sing or chant poetry, who believed that love was suicidal for women, should, in the end—" Radha left her sentence incomplete.

My curiosity increased. I asked, "What happened? Did she get married?"

"No, but . . . " Radha whispered in my ear, with a look of imparting a great secret. "She had a baby."

So that was it. But things were still not sorted out in my mind.

When Bhanumathi Amma left for her new place of work, Radha had gone to see her off. They met a worker going to the same place and she traveled with him. She seemed very happy. She was being accorded national recognition, for only workers of excellence were appointed to the kind of position she had been given. A woman from Kerala had been elevated to the front ranks. She insisted that all she wanted was for the sadanam to do well, and promised to return soon. Both wept as she left. Bhanu's first letter from the ashram expressed disappointment. She sounded homesick, and uneasy at being so far away. She felt ill, physically and mentally. The food must have disagreed with her for she threw up occasionally. She wrote, "Women are an accursed race, Radha! How weak, how unfortunate, we are! A single mistake can shatter the hopes and ambitions of a lifetime, destroy all the good in one. And yet, wouldn't it be wrong to correct one mistake by committing a second one?"

Radha was worried. It was not like Bhanumathi Chechi to make such profound statements, or to sound so depressed. She had been such a force in the sadanam, with her insistence on following a path of stern virtue, on never being swayed by emotion. She had always valued strength and despised weakness. How had she come to write like this? Did the letter simply reflect the unpleasantness of her surroundings?

Anxious to find out how things really were with Bhanumathi Chechi, Radha decided to look for a job in the area. She wrote to people she knew and sent applications for vacancies advertised in the newspapers. Finally her steady efforts over eight months brought her the summons to an interview. When she arrived, she went directly to the ashram and learnt that Bhanumathi Amma had left about two months ago. The sour-faced, middle-aged woman, who was evidently not from Kerala, smiled contemptuously, "She's ill, and people in her condition are not allowed to stay here. You may find her in a hospital or in a home for destitutes."

Radha went on, "I was so distressed. I had to find her, my Bhanu Chechi, my friend. The goddess I had been willing to die for." She paused, then hurried through the rest of the story. "I found her at last, Sister—in a hospital veranda, leaning against a pillar, clutching a new-born baby—an emaciated, withered woman. She was no longer the Bhanumathi Chechi we had worshipped. There was nothing to distinguish her from the thousands of women one saw everywhere. My idol had fallen and was shattered.

"I returned home on the next train. And got married."

Radha would soon have to alight. Neither of us spoke. There seemed nothing more to talk about. I had never thought of Bhanumathi Chechi as infallible or divine. After all, none of us are goddesses. Why cannot we overcome this contempt for natural human emotions? Why cannot we dare to be different? Reaching out to Bhanumathi Chechi and all others like her, I cry out:

> "Dearest friend! Sister! Look, why are you ashamed of a mistake you committed unknowingly? We who fight against wrongdoings must also learn to tolerate and forgive those who make mistakes. Who are we anyway to determine 'right' and 'wrong'? Why can't you forgive yourselves? Won't you come back to this glowing field of action? Come, let us walk together again toward a new awakening . . . And then let us write down that unforgettable name for posterity. These bits of paper are meant for that purpose. The pen is in your hand."

1958

NOTES

1. It is evident from the form of address that the narrator is not very close to Bhanumathi and speaks of her, with formality, as "Amma." Radha, who is like a friend and a sister, says "Chechi."
2. The place where Bhanumathi and the other members lived and worked.
3. One of Kerala's best-loved poets, Changampuzha Krishna Pillai (1911–1943) who wrote lyrical and romantic poetry.

Daughter of Humanity

MANUSHYAPUTRI

11

I T WAS THREE O'CLOCK when he arrived home, after a long and exhausting journey. There was a committee meeting at four, a public meeting at five, some important interviews between six-fifteen and seven, and, after that, someone to visit. He was aghast to find a crowd waiting to see him in the anteroom. Why did they not realize that he was a human being, and not made of stone or steel? How could he hope to complete the tasks he had set himself, when each minute contained only sixty seconds? He was always in a hurry, rushing to keep pace. He thought maybe he should never have started this marathon race.

As he collapsed into his office chair, he found that he had a severe headache. It occurred to him that he had not had time to bathe or eat that day. In any case, he always found it difficult to organize his day. He would eat, sleep, and rest whenever he could, that was all. There was hardly any time to spend with the little child whose arrival he had awaited with such great longing. As the leader of a political party, he had to be at the service of the public. He was aware that he had to endure certain discomforts and inconveniences in exchange for the pleasures and privileges of his position. That was why, when he entered the reception room, he controlled his irritation, smiled pleasantly, and talked to everyone, as he was expected to do.

But when his secretary brought him the names of those who were waiting to see him, he lost his temper. "Tell those idlers that I have no time for anyone today. I don't feel well. Besides, I don't usually see people at this hour. Ask them to come back tomorrow morning."

The secretary smiled to himself and waited patiently. He knew that his chief would see all of them and listen to what they had to tell him before he had lunch. It was possible that he would even forego lunch in order to get to the meeting on time. After all, that was how he had risen to his position as chief of the party. And that was exactly what happened. When the last visitor left the office, the secretary came and said softly, "There's a woman waiting to see you. She looks very poor and has come from quite far away. I did not bring her in earlier because she said she wanted to see you alone."

The man banged the table angrily. An ink bottle overturned and papers flew wildly.

"Do you want to kill me? Tell her that I'm human, I'm tired, ask her to come tomorrow. I don't care who she is. It's four-thirty and I'm late—"

The secretary responded quietly and respectfully, "I think that would be unkind. She arrived very early this morning and has not eaten a morsel all day. She's tired, she's walked a long way. All she wants is to see you for a minute. She said she'll go away at once."

He looked indifferently at the person who moved the expensive curtain aside and followed his secretary into the room. What an odd creature! She was completely enveloped in a *mundu* and held an old worn palm-leaf umbrella. Her long earlobes dangled[1] as she walked. She cowered back into a corner of the big room, looking like a character who had stepped out of an eighteenth-century story book. A little seven-year-old boy clung to her knees.

The leader was puzzled. There seemed something familiar about the woman, some likeness that evoked an image from the past, but he was not quite certain. Suddenly, he rose from his chair. The visitor continued to wait quietly, her eyes fixed on the ground.

He tried not to let his impatience show and spoke gently. "Please sit down. Where do you come from? I'm terribly rushed today. Tell me quickly, whatever it is that you have come to say."

The visitor raised her head. The mundu which covered her head slid down and he could see her face. She was trembling and looked confused, frightened. Her eyes brimmed with tears. She said very softly, "No, Govindankutty, I don't want to sit down. I'll go away now. I just wanted to catch a glimpse of you, that's all. I think you haven't quite recognized me, Govindankutty. Yes, I know I've changed, but—"

She obviously found it difficult to speak. He suddenly noticed a familiar scar on her forehead, made by years of daily obeisance to the rising sun, and the mark left on her wrists by bell metal bangles. An exclamation escaped him, "My God, Kunhathol Amma!"

They stared at each other. He read in her eyes the intensity of a mother who had been separated from her son for a long time, but her gaze held no reproach, no complaint. All it seemed to express was a belief in the reality and gentleness of love. It was as if his whole life was unfolding before him in that moment.

The party leader forgot his duties in the presence of the pitiful, shabbily dressed woman whom he had tried to turn away a little while ago. A great sense of guilt swept over him, the weight of sorrow oppressed him. It was as if an image that he worshipped every day had fallen from its pedestal. He felt confused. After all, an image was made of stone, and stone was incapable of experiencing joy or sorrow. Yet, stone was brittle. Why should he be shocked that it had broken? He thought, I fought to destroy these idols. But when I trampled on their broken fragments, I never once thought of the innocent victims trapped under them. Poor things! They were hurt, but their wounds had not bled and their cries of pain had been soundless. They had died of starvation, but had never begged for even a grain of rice. And here was one of the meek creatures that had been placed as an offering in the great sacrifice of which he had been a part, pouring her affection over him in a nectar-sweet benediction.

He felt himself shrink before her, this woman who had suffered so deeply. He felt that he was no longer the party leader who spoke at public gatherings, or the expert who was invited to committee meetings. He became a little boy again, a lively little boy in a faraway village, who picked fallen mangoes from the ground, played village games with his companions, dived and swam in the tanks. His father had died when he was very young and his uncles had abandoned the widow and his children. It was his mother who had struggled to keep them from starving. She had wanted to educate him, to set him up in life, but had not been sure how she would ever manage it. He was a bright child, and went through primary school with ease.

Kunhathol Amma had often said to his mother, "Don't worry about Govindankutty. He's a clever boy and will do well."

Amma would answer sadly, "How will I send him to school, Kunhathol? I can barely manage to feed him. If he goes to school, he'll need books, pencils, notebooks."

Kunhathol had looked thoughtful. "We'll find a way, Lakshmi. Tell him to collect flowers for my prayers everyday. I'll find him the money."

She looked at him now with the face of a compassionate Devi. She had always reminded him of the Devi, perhaps because he had encountered her most often at the temple, or because he always remembered her holding out a ball of rice to him, like Annapurna.[2] Every morning, he combed the woods and the hillside for flowers for her prayers. He was always ravenously hungry by the time he reached the *illam*. The little ones would have finished breakfast. Kunhathol would mix curd and mango pickle with rice, roll it into balls, and hand them to him, the bell metal bangles tinkling on her pale wrists. Those were the only occasions when he had eaten his fill.

Kunhathol's voice was sweeter than the delicious food. Whenever Amma wept, Kunhathol would say to her, "Don't cry, Lakshmikutty! He'll be all right. Wait and see, he'll make sure that Thazhathedath House has a tiled roof when he grows up."

Thazhathedath House's roof had been tiled, but Lakshmikutty had not lived to see it.

Kunhathol had been the child's only refuge after his mother died. She had poured her affection unstintedly over the destitute child. She often gave him money, and always kept aside sweets for him from the offerings to the deity, warning him not to show them to her own son, who, she said, had already eaten enough.

Kunhathol did not regard these gestures as simply a part of her spiritual duties. They were for her a necessary part of her everyday life. She seemed to exist in order to give. Neither she, nor those who partook of her generosity, thought this extraordinary. Everyone, Christians, Muslims, the lower castes, took whatever she gave unquestioningly, as if they had a right to it.

In the evenings, someone would call from the gate of the illam, "Does anyone need an evening meal?" There was always a response. The villagers took it for granted that the house was open to them all the time and that its granary and dining room were public. Govindankutty felt this way too. When he finished school and left the village, he did not think it necessary to say goodbye to Kunhathol. He had grown up by then, and started to read a great deal. He had learned enough about caste disputes to feel that emotions like affection, a sense of indebtedness, or gratitude, were misplaced and insincere.

The young Govindankutty fulfilled Kunhathol's predictions. Brilliant, but also fortunate, he soon became a success on public platforms and a valuable member of many groups. Years passed and he began to forget his old village. Great changes took place. People ceased to be shocked when the impossible happened.

A few days ago, on his way to a function, Govindankutty had driven past the house. The area where the great sixteen-pillared hall had stood was overgrown with weeds and thorns. The tank had dried up, and its walls had crumbled. The facade of the tiled outhouse at the gate pitched forward dangerously. The people with him had said, "This illam was ruined by its own generosity. The family refused to acknowledge the fact that times had changed. Visitors continued to be made welcome, no matter how many there were, or what time they arrived. When the tenant farmers no longer handed over the income from the land or even the taxes, the family began to sell the land in order to buy rice. When this source was also exhausted, they had to borrow money. They removed and sold the wooden rafters of the building so that they could fulfill what they believed were their charitable duties. Five hundred *paras* of rice were cooked for the senior namboodiri's funeral feast. Finally, the illam was sold to clear the debt they had incurred for the ceremonies. The older son was stricken with arthritis. The younger one had finished school, but could not find a job, and had joined a political party. An old tenant who felt sorry for Kunhathol had arranged for her to move with her invalid son and his children to a small house which had once been part of the family property, some distance away."

Govindankutty's throat constricted. He had demonstrated, shouted slogans, and worked actively to destroy the tyranny of the landholders. But here it had disintegrated by itself.

He had thought then that he would go and see Kunhathol Amma and find out how she was. He had wondered what life was like for her now. She used to starve herself regularly, even in the old days. Counting Ekadashi, Pradosham, and every Monday, she fasted almost twenty days in the month. Yet, on all these days, she cooked for and served others. With a smile on her drawn face, weakened by prolonged fasting, she would sing:

"Victory to you, who joyfully serve
Generous helpings to vast gatherings
Beautiful one, daughter of the mountains,
Mother of Cherukunnu, victory to you!"

One day, his mother had said to her, "Kunhathol Amma, we have no choice. We starve because we do not have enough to eat. Why do you starve?"

Kunhathol answered, "Because I want to experience hunger, Lakshmi, and because I want to share the sorrow of those who are in need. Poverty is a terrible thing! I cannot bear to think of children crying with hunger and not being able to give them food. Bhagavan! Guruvayurappan! Please don't let anyone suffer so."

When she folded her hands in prayer, you would want to pray too. And this generous woman who had given endlessly of her prosperity, was now—

His head reeled. The car waiting to take him to the meeting

sounded its horn. The secretaries looked in impatiently.

They had not spoken, the mother and her "son," but they had understood each other perfectly.

At last, Kunhathol said, "Forgive me, Govindankutty, for having bothered you. Lakshmikutty entrusted you to me before she died. I am so glad for you. I feel as happy as if you were my own son, Unni."

She stopped, then continued very hesitantly, "Unni has been bedridden for the last eight years. The illam is in ruins. The younger one finished his studies and tried to find a job. They tell me that upper-caste people no longer have a right to education or to employment. Anyway, he left home. I hear that he spends his time going to meetings and making public speeches. Unni has a daughter old enough to be married, Everyone said you would help, Govindankutty—"

She pushed her grandson forward and spoke so softly that he could barely hear, "If you can help us send this child to school, he would at least get a meal at noon. Bhagavan! Guruvayurappan! Protect us!"

He froze, inexpressibly shocked. That Annapurneswari herself should have to beg for an afternoon meal for her little grandson! Her charity had borne no fruit. The fortress of aristocracy lay shattered at his feet.

Tears ran down his face. He bent, touched the dust of her feet, and said, "Forgive me, Amme, forgive me! Govindankutty is a sinner. He is cruel and ungrateful. And yet you do not curse him. It was we who destroyed your illam, we who took away the income from your land. We fought for the cause of the starving, but forgot the hands that had once served us food. And yet, you do not find fault with us. You envelop us in a blessing more powerful than a curse.

"I do not know if I can ever bring your younger son back to you. I cannot even guarantee the noon meal for the child. But I have something to ask of you. Please be a mother to motherless Govindankutty. May the next generation inherit the love, the affection, the innocence that is your nature and that I have never encountered in anyone else."

He told the secretary, "Take my mother to the car. Then telephone and tell them that I cannot come for today's meeting. I have duties that I cannot shirk. I am a human being too, and the son of a woman!"

1960

NOTES

1. See Introduction, p.xiv.
2. The Devi in the form of the generous giver.

The Boon

VARAM

12

"M ATAJI IS on her way to the ashram. They said there will be special prayers and worship of the deity today and bhajans will be sung afterwards."

"And so?"

"Mukunda Menon brought her over for his son's anna prasanam.[1] He was determined that she should be present. You have to admit that it's quite amazing. It was certainly Mataji's blessing that worked this miracle. Mukunda Menon is forty-five years old, and his wife is forty. Imagine having one's first baby at forty. If Mataji wills it, anything is possible."

So that was it. "You want to see Amma as well and ask her for a boon. You want to be a mother. I've seen innumerable Matajis like this one, my dear!" He wanted to remind her about the doctors she had consulted. They had not been able to do anything for her. But he kept quiet. It would be cruel. She would cry. He might cry as well. After all, sorrow was not her exclusive right. They had been married for fifteen years, and had no children. The various courses of treatment they had tried had all failed. His wife now felt that their only hope lay in pilgrimages and offerings to temples. He had no faith in these things. But then, do we only do things we have faith in? It would be wonderful if the Yogini Mata blessed them and they did have a child. If it did not happen, he would not grieve.

"All right then, we'll go. After all, she is a woman, and old enough to be my mother. Besides, my mother is dead. Yes, let's go and see her. But I will not touch her feet, nor ask her for a boon. I'll come to keep you company, that's all."

That was enough to make her happy. And he was curious about the ashram, he wanted to find out what they did there. It was one of the city's best known establishments. The Yogini Mata had innumerable disciples, many of whom were in high positions. All longed to lay down their burdened sorrowing bodies, wrapped in Banares silks and synthetic materials, and rest from their toil. Some of the devotees wanted to have children, others sought better positions than they already held, or solutions to family disputes. Still others wanted to be cured of diseases. There were some who came merely because they were curious. Most had faith in Mataji and looked upon her as Jaganmata, the Mother of the Universe, a deity to be worshipped. Their deep faith moved him, even though he believed that it was unreasoning and blind.

The ashram and its vicinity were beautifully decorated. Glowing lights filled the hall. On the raised platform in the center was a full-length portrait of Amma with flowers heaped before it. The flames of a sacred oil lamp gleamed bright, and the fragrance of camphor and incense filled the air. The Yogini Mata sat in meditation. She wore a bright ochre silk saree and a coral chain around her neck. Her eyes were half-closed. She sat in the yogic padmasana posture, her palms resting upturned on her thighs. In the radiance of the lamps around her, she shone like an image of gold. It was impossible not to imagine her as the Devi. Her light radiated to every part of the hall. Disciples showered flowers over her.

> "*Tarakanthi tiraskari*
> *Nasabharana bhasura.*"
> ("Her nose ring set with a shining jewel
> Brighter than the planet Venus.")

The lines from the "Lalitha Sahasranamam"[2] resounded through the room.

Suma joined the devotees in worship and was soon lost in a transport of faith. Everyone seemed to be in something of a trance. As for him, he could not stop looking at Mataji, although he was not sure what he was searching for. How old would she be, this woman thousands worshipped? Fifty? Sixty? Maybe she was only forty-five. She held the vast gathering of people by the sheer force of their overwhelming desire for happiness. For some reason, the Yogini Mata made him think of two of the world's best known prime ministers. Did she make him think of another woman who had the same extraordinary sense of authority? Whatever it was, he decided that he was too much of a materialist to surrender to this woman's magical power.

Around him, people began to shout. He realized that Amma was emerging from her meditation. She took great handfuls of flowers and poured them over her head, as if in a state of ecstasy.

The devotees cried, "Jaya Mata, Jaya Mata—"

Flowers fell like rain. The chanting of prayers grew louder. Mataji got up and raised her right hand, her gesture as delicate as a dancer's. "*Swasthir bhavathu . . . Swasthi, swasthi,*" "May all good things be with you."

She laid her hand on the head of each devotee in blessing, gave them flowers and *prasadam*. The kindness and compassion in her eyes were like a caress. She got down from the platform, and came forward. He suddenly realized that he was the only person in the room who had not prostrated before her. Was she coming toward him, the unbeliever? Was the Yogini Mata really the Devi?

She placed flowers and prasadam in his hand, bent forward, and called him, "Son—"

He looked at her. Those eyes, that voice, the radiance of her look. Did a diamond nose ring glitter in her right nostril, or was it the starbright light in her eyes that blinded him? He felt himself grow pale, his limbs become weak. Who was this? Whom did she look like? He wanted to call her "Meena Mami"[3] and put his arms around her. What an amazing likeness! Meena Mami! Where are you now? Could you have become Yogini Mata? I can't believe it.

Amma circled his head with flowers and vermilion, and laid her hand firmly on him in blessing: "Son! I am your mother. May your desires be fulfilled. May you have faith and prosperity." In the moment's silence that followed, he was conscious of intense happiness.

His eyes filled. Were they tears of devotion or of faith? He found himself prostrate before her.

"*Swasthi! Swasthi!*"

Enough, Amme. My soul has been satisfied. When did you take Meena Mami's form, Amme? Where is Mami now? Grant her peace! I lie prostrate before you, this person named Gopakumar, whom they call Unni at home. I do not want children. Give Meena Mami's children back to her. Grant her peace.

He closed his eyes, lost in the power of her touch, and prayed.

His faith gave his wife great happiness. His friends were astonished—the rationalist had turned into a devotee! So that is what he really was, the rest had been a facade. All right, my friends. I don't care what you think. And none of you know Meena Mami's story, anyway. I'll not tell you. I'll keep it to myself, like a blessing meant exclusively for me.

When they came back home, his wife said, "Did you see how charismatic Amma is? Even you have become a different person. I'm sure we will have children now. The Devi is great."

His reply was strangely brusque. "I don't want to have children. I prayed that we may not have any."

She began to weep. "Now that you've said that, it will become true. You take everything too frivolously. But this is serious. We saw the Devi's strength for ourselves."

"I don't know much about the Devi's power, but I do know Meena Mami's. She never made offerings to a temple. She never prayed. Yet she had four fine sons, strong, beautiful boys! And what use was it? They brought her limitless sorrow. If one has no children, all one regrets is not having them. What is the point of having children who make you unhappy all the time? Poor Meena Mami! If you listen to her story, you'll never want to have children. Sit down, let me tell it to you."

"I was about eight at the time. We lived in a big city in the north, my parents and I. None of our neighbors were from Kerala. They spoke Hindi, Gujarati, Marathi. My mother, who had grown up in rural Kerala, did not know any of these languages and found it hard to make friends. So she stayed at home all the time, and we had no contact with our neighbors. Until one day a new family came to the flat next door. There were two cartfuls of luggage, four little boys, Meena Mami and her husband. Once they arrived, the neighborhood became extremely lively.

"As soon as they came, Meena Mami swept and mopped all the floors in every room of the house, and lit an oil lamp. She drew a kolam, a design with rice flour, outside the front door. The clothes-lines grew heavy with silk sarees and baby clothes. Polished vessels of brass and silver shone on the shelves. The smell of dosais, idlis and halva filled the air.

"The eldest son, Sundaram, was a fine football player. He had won many trophies both at school and at college. Meena Mami arranged them neatly in the showcase in her drawing room.

"Murthy, the second, had a passion for reading. He read out English poems to us beautifully and wrote a few himself. Indeed, it was the enthusiasm Murthy and I shared for poetry that brought us together.

"Ambi had a gift for drawing. Meena Mami scolded him continually because he sketched on the walls and on the floors that she wiped so spotlessly clean.

"Chinnaswami had just begun to hum the first notes, *sa-ri*—

"They all obeyed Meena Mami unquestioningly. She made decisions for everyone. If anyone had asked me at the time who God was, Sume, I would unhesitatingly have said, 'Meena Mami'! She was so beautiful. Her fair-skinned face was always flushed and beaded with sweat. Her hair was curly. She wore vermilion on her forehead, diamonds in her ears and a nose ring with three brilliant stones in her right nostril. I loved watching her nose ring glitter when she moved or laughed. My father must have felt this way too, for whenever Meena Mami smiled, I would hear him chant the line from the "Lalitha Sahasranamam" softly, under his breath:

"Tarakanthi tiraskari
Nasabharana bhasura."

"Meena Mami's husband was tall, pale, and thin. Meena Mami ruled over the poor man, a *vedantin* by nature, as she ruled over the children and us, her neighbors. Amma would say: 'She was born to rule. What an efficient woman she is,' Amma would tell us. 'How confident and capable! And so beautiful too! Look at Meena Mami's children, fool, and learn to be like them.'

"I never expressed aloud the thought that Amma was not as clever as Meena Mami. I must confess that I nursed a faint regret that I was not Meena Mami's son, and tried to make up for it by being friends with Murthy. I obeyed Meena Mami's every command and listened devotedly to her every word. Astonishingly, Meena Mami thought I was cleverer than Murthy. She would say to him, 'Learn to be like Unni,' and I would feel so proud. She always offered me a share of all the delicacies she gave Murthy to eat, dropping them into my hands so that she did not touch me. So the days went by.

"Meena Mami wanted her sons to excel in everything they did. Sundaram held the first rank in the Intermediate examination. He had studied physics, chemistry, and biology and enrolled without difficulty in the medical college. Murthy and I started on an English Honours course. Meena Mami had decided that Murthy would be a professor and Ambi an engineer. Chinnaswami would of course train to be a musician since he had a talent for music. Meena Mami's uncle had been a well-known musician, and Chinnaswami would keep the line alive. Besides, bhagavathars or musicians made a considerable amount of money nowadays. Meena Mami had made up her mind about everyone's future.

"However, all Meena Mami's careful plans were foiled. Her eldest son, Sundaram, was a handsome and gifted young man. The girls in the college found him enormously attractive. There was a rumor that he had fallen in love with one of them, a pretty girl from a different community. As soon as it reached Meena Mami's ears, she took him to their village and persuaded him to marry a wealthy executive's daughter, who brought him a rich dowry of fifteen thousand rupees, jewels made from a hundred sovereigns, and a large collection of silver vessels. But Sundaram refused to go back to college after his marriage. He grew silent and moody and became seriously disturbed. He finally ran away from home.

"Murthy said, 'It all happened because my eldest brother is far too gentle. She could never have made me do what he did. Just let her try.'

"Amma said, 'Of course she can force you to do what she wants, Murthy. If Meena Mami makes up her mind, nothing can change it. She was born to rule.'

"'It's not for nothing I'm her son,' retorted Murthy. 'Like her, I shall do exactly as I please. Wait and see.'

"Meena Mami expected great things from Murthy. He would be a writer, a public speaker, and the ideal of the young people of the city. Even if he did not become the prime minister, everyone thought he had the skills, the potential, to become at least a minister of state. But these hopes proved illusory.

"As if to avenge the injustice that his mother had meted out to his elder brother, Murthy brought home a Muslim girl, pretending she was his classmate. Meena Mami drove her out of the house. Murthy retaliated by marrying her. The couple took a boat to Pakistan and never came back.

"When friends came to commiserate with her about her reckless sons, Meena Mami displayed an astonishing indifference. She did not weep or lament. She did not betray the slightest sign of irritation. She went on with her routine as usual, washed and mopped the floors, drew a kolam at the front door, and served her puzzled visitors vadais, halva, and coffee.

"'What a courageous woman! She's lost two fine, strong sons, and look at her. In her place, I would have collapsed,' said Amma.

"I no longer went to the house after Murthy left. I was convinced that Meena Mami had driven him away. That was what people said, anyway, both in private and in public.

"I completed my studies and found a fairly good job in Kerala. When I was about to leave, Amma said, 'Go and ask Meena Mami for her blessing, otherwise things will never go well with you.'

"She was reading the Bhagavad Gita when I went in. She said, without raising her eyes from the book, 'It's Unni, isn't it?'

"'Yes. I've got a job, in Kerala. Please give me your blessing, Meena Mami. If I have ever done anything to offend you, intentionally, or unknowingly—'

"I did not want to acknowledge the fact that my voice trembled, so I bent down quickly, touched her feet, and then my forehead. I had never touched anyone's feet before.

"Meena Mami got up and put her arms around me. She caressed my hair and said, 'All will go well with you, Unni. Your mother is gentle and good. Good fortune will bless her. Take care never to give her pain.'

"Meena Mami laid both her hands firmly on my head and gave me her blessing. Her nose ring quivered. Her eyes shone bright, her cheeks grew pale. But she was dry eyed and quite composed. Neither of us spoke of those who were lost to her, although their presence filled the space around us.

"I never saw Meena Mami again. Occasionally I heard little bits of news about her. She had deliberately denied Ambi an education, found him a modest job in the city, and taken care to get him married early. Her new daughter-in-law was exactly like Meena Mami herself, a woman born to rule. She quarreled with her mother-in-law, took all the family jewelry, and went away to her own house, taking her husband with her.

"Chinnaswami's docile wife's uncle said to Meena Mami, 'They've all deserted you. Give whatever you have left to Chinnaswami. He'll look after you.'

"Meena Mami scorned the idea of buying affection in this manner. She sold all her possessions, gave the proceeds to a charitable institution, and went on a pilgrimage with her husband. She must be exercising her authority now over the devotees with her. She must have turned into an image of sorrow draped in ochre.

"So you see, Sume, this is why I told you that I do not wish to have children. We can live happily as Meena Mami's disciples, or the Yogini Mata's. I know how deeply Meena Mami cared for her children. But she wanted those she loved to be her slaves. One day, Sume, she is sure to become a slave to the people she loves, and she will caress them then as she caressed me today. Poor Meena Mami! No one understood her. Not even I.

"Amme! Mataji! Grant my Meena Mami peace! Grant her a tranquil mind! The devotee named Gopakumar, who is called Unni at home, prays for this. Grant serenity and peace of mind to all sorrowing mothers."

1962

NOTES

1. The ceremony in which a baby is given rice for the first time.
2. The thousand names of the Devi (Lalitha), a part of the *Brahmanda Puranam*.
3. "Mami" is the Tamil word for aunt.

Fulfillment

SAPHALYAM

13

HAD THE GUESTS in the northern *pandal* been served? It was time to make coffee for those who were seated in the middle room. Had the guests in the inner hall been given *tamboolam*? Amma tried to be everywhere—she had to attend to every detail, she had to supervise as well as organize. She must take care to say a few words to every person who came. Last time there had been complaints, and there would not be an occasion like this for a long time. It wasn't easy, making sure that everything was just right.

She gave orders, whirled in and out of the house. The harsh reality suddenly turned her heart over when Mini came to say good-bye, still in her bridal attire, her wedding garland knotted over her right hand. Today was her daughter's wedding! Mini was married now, and about to go away, become part of another family. Her adored youngest child.

She pretended to have no such thoughts and looked at Mini. What a lovely bride she was. Were they tears of joy, or of the sadness of departure, that she saw in the long, moist, wide eyes? Sreedevi Amma laid her hand on her daughter's shoulder and then suddenly sat down because she could not bear it. Mini knelt and touched her mother's feet. When Sreedevi Amma placed her hands on Mini's head in blessing, it seemed as if her whole life flowed into them.

Mini's face was flushed and her eyes were misted. Her chest heaved and fell as if she had to hold a strong emotion in check. She touched her mother's feet, then her own forehead, and rose. Neither said a word. Even their tears seemed to hold themselves back in deference to the occasion.

"You must start now, Mini, before the auspicious period is over," said her father. "Rahu kalam[1] will soon begin. Everyone is ready to leave."

Mini looked at her father, her eyes filled with tears, and walked slowly away. Neither said goodbye. The formulae of parting seemed too inadequate. If she bent down now and touched her father's feet, what if her pent-up emotions exploded?

The car waited at the entrance and the bride and bridegroom climbed in. Mini turned back once, as if she wanted to draw the image of the house where she had been born into her eyes. Then she pulled the edge of her wedding sari over her face and bent her head. Sreedevi Amma wanted to cry out, "Don't cry, child, please don't cry—" but she did not say anything. Immersed in her thoughts, she waited till the car turned the bend in the road. Then she quickly wiped away her tears, taking care that no one saw her, and hurried back into the house.

The familiar routine again. Where was the key to the cupboard? Was there coffee for everyone? The poor were being fed now. She must make sure that they were served plenty of *payasam*. There was so much she had to attend to.

The bustle continued till the evening by which time most of the guests had left. Sreedevi Amma went to the bedroom to rest. Her eldest son was packing his things. She asked, "Do you really have to leave tomorrow, Kuttan?"

"How can I stay longer, Amme? I've only five days left, and I have to spend four of them in the train. They won't give me a day more because of the emergency."

Her eldest daughter was leaving as well. Her husband had not come with her since the children could not miss school. No one had time to spare. Everyone was terribly busy. How complicated life had become!

Sreedevi Amma had wanted to suggest that one of the grand-children live with her. But there were no English-medium schools in this rural area, nor nursery schools with ayahs. Ah well, as long as they were all right, wherever they were. She saw them off without tears or protests. The wedding guests had left. The pandal was dismantled. Only a faint scent of withered jasmine and perfume lingered.

She felt lonely for the first time in her life. As if she had forgotten something, lost something. She wandered aimlessly through the empty rooms. Everything lay in confusion. Mini's veena that used to stand against the wall was no longer there, although her sewing machine was. There were vermilion stains on the mirror. A photograph of Mini in a dance pose hung on the wall. It had been taken ten years ago, at the school anniversary. Mini had been passionately fond of sports. How often had she scolded the child for being wild and boyish.

Someone had hung a little toy aeroplane by a silk thread on one of the blades of the fan. Deepu, perhaps? He was such a naughty little boy. Like Unni. His grandmother spoiled him a great deal, this eldest son of her eldest son. She removed the plane and tried to straighten it. She did not understand the mechanism of these newfangled toys.

Reshmi's little dress lay under the cot. It looked grimy and dusty. They must have forgotten to take it with them. Reshmi's mother was so careless. Sreedevi Amma reached out for the dress and sniffed it. It felt like the cheeks of the adorable little girl. She could see her now as she ran in, after her bath, still wet, the curls on her forehead flying.

She heard a footstep outside and hurried to see who it was. An old beggar. She gave him a coin and watched him leave. Poor man! Perhaps he did not have a home, or children of his own. Perhaps they had all grown up. Sreedevi Amma sighed.

The household chores were done. The servants had left. The house was silent and deserted. Harvested fields lay around it. A

cow lowed for a missing calf. Sreedevi Amma thought how on evenings like this when the children came back from school, they
loved to tumble in the white sand of the courtyard. They would
scamper all over the kitchen, the bedrooms, and the attic, till they
wore her patience out. One of them would hit another, both would
cry, and the others would hoot with laughter. What an uproar they
used to make! There were occasions when Sreedevi Amma would
hold her head in her hands and lament, "Guruvayurappan! These
little sparrows make my head spin with their clamor!"

Life had been a ruthless heaving sea in those days. Caught in
the ebb and flow of duty, she was always busy and worked tirelessly, day and night. There may have been goals she had wanted
to reach—what were they? Had she achieved them? Sreedevi
Amma searched her soul.

Her first baby was born within a year of her marriage. She had
said to her husband, holding the little one close to her, "Let's make
Unni a doctor."

"Why not an engineer?" Unni's father laughed, as he always did.
He could never be serious about anything. His mind was as un-
cluttered as a child's!

In spite of Sreedevi Amma's dream, Unni became neither a doctor nor an engineer. He worked in a government concern in a distant town.

She had wanted Shoba to become a great musician. But Shoba
had forgotten all her music now, and lived quietly and contentedly
with her husband, a college professor.

Revi and Rema lived abroad. They had won distinctions in the
subjects they had chosen to study. They wrote occasionally. It was
Mini who usually replied to them. Mini often said to her mother,
"Let them all go away, Amme, my older brothers and sisters. I'll
stay with you. I'll never leave you."

Mini did well at her studies, but had not wanted to work. And
then, of course, she did marry. Her husband seemed to have much
in common with her. When Sreedevi Amma saw them seated together in the wedding hall, her own happiness had moved her to
tears.

"Be happy, Mini! May both of you know great happiness. We feel fulfilled."

They had moved to their own home after the *tarawad* was partitioned. The only possessions they had at the time were five small children and a stretch of barren land; all demanded attention and had to be tended with care. The earth required seed and manure, the little ones needed love and schooling. Failing to provide either of these needs was to fail to provide both. Sreedevi Amma and her husband worked ceaselessly. Her obstinate determination that the children should do well became an obsession. If Unni scored a single mark less than she had calculated, she would first hit him and then lament, striking her forehead. She had pawned her jewels and vessels on occasion, or mortgaged the land to pay their school fees. And so those days had passed. The children were independent now, and she did not have to worry about them anymore. Everything seemed wonderful on the surface.

For the first time in her life, that day, she was aware of a piercing sense of the sadness of things. Happiness was an illusion, it did not exist. The worries, the obsessions, the heartaches that had been part of the race for happiness were, in reality, true joy. The days when work piled up. The nights she could not sleep. The lack of money. The excitement with which she waited for the results of the examinations. If only the obligations one owed one's children were never fulfilled!

The heady scent of jasmine wafted in with the evening air. If Mini had been here, she would have plucked every flower, to make a garland. She would have scattered flowers all over the floor and even tucked a strand in her mother's greying hair. Sreedevi Amma hated to see the flowers plucked. She preferred to have them open out fully on their stems. But Mini would argue, "Why does a plant need flowers, Amme? They'll have withered by tomorrow. See, how good they look on our hair, how sweet they smell!"

It was true. Flowers withered so quickly on a plant, and then, one could no longer smell them. And yet, when Sreedevi Amma saw the jasmine denuded of all its buds, she could not help it, she felt unhappy. It seemed to her like a mother separated from her children.

Today, however, when she went to the jasmine bower, she unthinkingly plucked a few buds. Oh, well, she could put them in the reading room. If she did not make this small concession, Mini's absence would drive her mad.

She heard a sudden outburst of laughter from the fields. Mini's father was on his way home. There was someone with him. This explosive laugh was his birthright. What a man! How could he bring himself to laugh today like an innocent child?

She had forgotten to make the Horlicks he usually drank at this time. Mini used to have it ready for him. The two of them clowned all the time like little children. And if she complained that he indulged his daughter too much, he would say, "Ah, Muthassi, you must excuse her. She's a child, and bound to be playful. Don't take it all so seriously."

Sreedevi Amma went to the kitchen to mix the Horlicks. Mini's father called out, "Mini's mother! Look, the mangoes have begun to ripen on The Smiling Mango Tree. I've plucked a couple for you. They smell wonderful!"

They had planted the mango tree the day Mini was born. It was she who had named it "The Smiling Mango Tree." They had put a swing up in its branches. Mini would go high up on it, breathe the fragrance of the blossoms, and chant, "Smiling Mango Tree, pour out your honey."

She remembered the times when the children sat up all night, to pluck the mangoes as soon as they were ripe. Windblown memories from the past lay scattered in the empty spaces underneath the tree.

Sreedevi Amma wiped her eyes and handed the Horlicks to her husband. She did not speak, but he knew. He chided her, affectionately, "Foolish girl! Why are you crying? Should we cry when our children go forward into their new lives?"

But she continued to sob. He caught her hand and held it close. "Do you remember, Mini's mother? It was forty years ago that we came here together. This was a forest at the time. We cleared it, planted fruit trees, tended them till they bore fruit. We had children. We brought them up, educated them, set them up in life.

And now we're alone once more. It's all for the best. Look at that nest there. It was crowded with eggs and little ones for a few days. I still remember how I watched you looking at the mother feed its young from her beak. The nest is empty now. But so many other birds have built their nests in our garden. Life is change, and we have to change too. And so, Mini's mother, I'll tell you what you must do now. Just like the poet Vylopilli[2] sang,

"Rub chunam on a betel leaf and give it to me.
Let us honor this auspicious night
With our own celebration."

Sreedevi Amma could not help it, she laughed through her tears. And then she saw that tears were also streaming down the laughing face of Mini's father.

1967

NOTES

1. Inauspicious periods, which are to be avoided. It is not advisable to set out on a journey or to undertake any task during this period.
2. The poet Vylopilli Sridhara Menon (1911–1985) started by writing in the romantic tradition of Changampuzha Krishna Pillai (1911–1943), his poems gaining great depth and complexity in his later years.

Dhirendu Majumdar's Mother

DHIRENDU MAJUMDARUDE AMMA 14

I WONDER whether you know who I am? My name is Shanti Majumdar. I am ninety years old. I was born in a small village in East Bengal, and I grew up there. I gave birth to nine children, seven boys and two girls. I sacrificed five of them for India and four for Pakistan.[1] Then I adopted a whole new generation as my children and grandchildren. I wanted to die in the country in which I was born. All my ancestors were born on its soil and ultimately became part of it. If the freedom fighters had not lifted Shanti Muthassi on their shoulders and brought her away, she would have fallen on the battlefield and attained her salvation with dignity.

You are surprised that I fear nothing? Why should I fear anything? After all, none of Shanti's children were cowards. India is my country. The bones of five of my children lie moldering here. But Shanti Muthassi did not want to come into this country as a foreigner and a refugee. Perhaps you find it difficult to understand, my children, that Bharat was not just a handful of earth to us. She was a divine mother, green and fertile, full of sweet fruits and clear water. We meditated on the thousands of swords shining in her hands, and we brought up our children. And then we gave up our children so that Bharat might be free. Have you heard of those brave unselfish soldiers, who lost their lives in the early years of the struggle for India's freedom? Do tales like theirs exist in the history you were taught?

Memories foam to the surface of my mind, and make my flesh tingle. They are memories not of one person, or of one family, they are memories of the pitiful story of an entire country. Shanti Majumdar's story will make this clear to you. Listen now . . . Our house was in the central region of what is now called East Pakistan. It was the zamindari, the large estate, that lay on the left side of the river Padma as it flowed eastward to the sea. Floods occurred frequently, and when they did, the villagers usually took shelter in the big hall behind the Durga temple in the village. The married women of the Majumdar family would, however, sit on the balcony of their elegant mansion and watch the waters of the Padma in their destructive dance. They never left the *antahpuram* and never met men other than their husbands. People used to recall how when the beloved wife of our younger uncle, Abani Majumdar, went into labor and was in excruciating pain, he wanted a doctor to be fetched from the town. But the eldest Majumdar, who also had the title of Raja Saheb, would not hear of it. Custom had decreed that if the women of the Majumdar household fell ill, the only man who would be permitted to enter the inner rooms was Kalan, the God of Death.

I was nine years old when I came into this household in a covered palanquin, dressed as a bride in red silk, with vermilion fresh in the parting of my hair. I never went out of the house again until I was fifty. When my eldest son, Dhirendu, was in college, he had begged me to go as far as the main entrance to the house, to meet one of his friends. Later, when the Governor Saheb and his wife visited us, my husband tried to persuade me to go and receive them. I never agreed to any such requests. It was unthinkable for women born in the second half of the nineteenth century to do so. We were shocked at the very idea of breaking rules. But what could we do when our own children began to break them?

When husbands take one side and children the other, how does one deal with the terrible conflict of ideals that results? Whose side does one take? How can you ever understand, my children, how agonizing such confrontations can be?

The Majumdar family was pro-British. We had lands and zamindaris in many areas. In addition, my husband was a Rai Bahadur, an honorary judge, and a member of the esteemed Advisory Committee to the British Government. The Governor and the Viceroy were frequent guests in our house. When our eldest son, Dhirendu, completed his B.A., we wanted him to join the Indian Civil Service. My husband said, "Rai Bahadur is only a title after all. If he joins the I.C.S., he will have wealth and authority."

As for Dhirendu, he went back and forth between Calcutta and our village, unaware of all the great plans for his future. He was handsome, a good student, and a man of few words. He was known and loved for his compassion. Often, he would gather a group of poor people around him, arrange for them to sleep in the stable, or in the dark room over the bathing tank, and have food sent over from the house. He used to ask me for large sums of money to help them. The praise heaped on Dhirendu fell sweetly on my ears.

One night, he brought a woman in purdah to the antahpuram. "Amme," he said, "this is an ascetic of the Bhairava sect. She has taken a vow of silence and will not speak to anyone. I want her to stay in the small room next to your prayer room. Don't allow the servants to serve her food, please serve her yourself."

How happy that made me! At an age when young men seek the company of women, here was Dhirendu offering an ascetic hospitality. The yogini sat in the little dark room, reading and scribbling all the time. Dhiren would take out huge bundles of paper from the room. They often sounded as if they were chanting mantrams together. Whenever I took them food, the woman would cover her face and move to a corner. I presumed she did this because I was not her disciple and she did not know me.

On a new moon night, when it was raining heavily and the river was in flood, Dhirendu called me, "The yogini is leaving today, Amme. She wants to see you and give you her blessing. Come—"

He pulled away the ochre robe that covered the yogini's face. I drew back, terrified. It was a young man! He could have been

Dhiren's elder brother, they looked so alike. He folded his hands and said, "Forgive me, Amme! I am Surya Sen.[2] They call me Masterda. We worship our motherland as Mahakali, with daggers and discs in each of her hundred hands, her hair drenched in the blood of her enemies, wearing a chain made of skulls. But today, for the first time, I have seen the Devi in her Annapurneswari form, as compassion incarnate. Bless me, that this image may be part of my meditation."

Masterda bent down, his tears flowing, and touched the dust of my feet. I wept too. Was this really Surya Sen, the famous revolutionary? He who had performed such awesome deeds! They called him a traitor to the country! The police force was frantically trying to track him down! My heart flowed into my hands, as I placed them on his head. "Surya Sen! No, Masterda! The mother who bore you must be my elder sister."

It was growing late. The boat lay waiting on the Padma. He climbed in with Dhiren. While I stood still, watching, the boat moved over the turbulent waters and was lost to sight. Shanti Majumdar, the woman of the antahpuram, died at that moment. A new Mother of Bengal was born.

Soon, I began to discover all that was happening in the country. But I pretended I knew nothing. I deliberately led two lives. A few days later, Surya Sen was apprehended by the police and sentenced to the gallows. When Dhirendu's father heard the news, he said, "Look at that. Now, traitors like him are sure to be punished in the end. They insist on making trouble for themselves. Do you know, just yesterday the Governor said to me, 'Your eldest son is a brave man, Majumdar Saheb! I've made up my mind to have him enrolled in the police.' "

I found it difficult to hold back my tears. Was I weeping for Surya Sen's death? Or at the thought of my son becoming a police commissioner? Oh, never mind. Dhiren continued to bring people in all sorts of disguises to the house, even after Masterda's death, and I gave them all shelter. But suddenly one day, the situation exploded. When the police chief told Rai Bahadur Niharendu Majumdar that his son was a wanted man and that they were searching for him everywhere, he came into the antahpuram and shouted, "No, I do not have a son like that. My eldest son is dead." Then he turned to me. "If that traitor comes here, I forbid you to give him even a mouthful of water to drink. He has to be handed over at once to the police," he ordered.

I listened, and, devoted and dutiful wife that I was, I still continued to help my son on many occasions. I gave him everything he asked for. Often, I pleaded with him, "My son, don't go on with this. Promise me you won't—"

Before he became involved in the Chittagong conspiracy,[3] Dhirendu said to me, "Do you know, Amme, that in ancient times, the mothers of Greece offered their eldest sons to the Goddess of War in sacrifice. To die for the land in which you were born is to attain salvation. You are Devi, Amme. Give up your eldest son for your motherland. You will still have eight children."

I began to cry. "A mother is greater than the country, my son. She has a heart and it will break. A country, after all, is only soil and stone."

Dhiren kissed my forehead. "No, Amme, no. A country is made up of millions of mother's hearts. Hearts that feel pain, that suffocate and weep. If I die for the freedom of this grieving country, you must sing 'Vande Mataram'[4] with a smile. Promise me that you'll smile, Amme!"

He touched the dust of my feet and sped away. News came later that he had died in a blast of dynamite during an attack on the arsenal. His father went insane with rage and grief. But I sang "Vande Mataram" in his father's hearing, weeping and laughing, screaming like a madwoman, louder and louder . . .

"You who wield sharp swords in your many hands—"

My children, I am so thirsty! My throat is parched, give me some water. Cold, cold water. Ah-h, that's enough. I should not have spoken of all this now. Or even thought of it. For I have become an outsider, a refugee, asking for your kindness. People have forgotten Dhirendu Majumdar long ago. Why should they remember his mother?

Dhiren's ghost haunted his younger brothers. Sharadindu, who had gone to London to become a barrister, shot an Englishman at the entrance to India House and then committed suicide. Nityendu and Satyendu would not go to college at all! Their father's health broke down, he became paralysed and bedridden. The lands were confiscated. And yet, children, the Majumdar house still remains famous. For it became a home for all the freedom fighters. Tarakeshwar was arrested in the cellar of the house. Ganesh Ghosh, Savitri, and Kalpana were all constant visitors. Have you heard of Preeti Wadeddar?[5] She was a close friend of my daughter Minati. Poor girl, she really did not have the makings of a revolutionary. The sight of blood made her feel faint and tears frightened her. Who would have believed that this was the girl who would throw a bomb at the European Club in Pahartali in Chittagong and then swallow potassium cyanide in order to escape capture? The freedom you now enjoy is soaked in their blood. Nityendu, Satyendu, and Minati did not live to see that freedom. The Congress party was established, and then came Gandhiji. When Gandhiji felt that Gopinath did not deserve a pardon,[6] I argued, "Bapuji, remember that history will not pardon you. Courage is not a crime. Our Bengali youths kill or die for their country and so become immortal."

At the end of it all, when the country was partitioned according to religion and community, Trailokya Chakraborty said to Nehru,[7] "Why did you decapitate Bengal? Who asked you to divide us? There is neither Hindu nor Muslim here. The Bengalis are one, and have always been so. If head and body are severed from each other, the very planets will take revenge. The sun and moon will be eclipsed! Wait and see!"

The eclipse has taken place and devoured everything! We too considered fleeing to India at the time of the partition. Then we wondered why should we do so. It was all the same, being here or there. If we served the country unitedly, we felt that all would go well, no matter where we were. And so we plunged into the service of the new nation. Once again, people gathered under the roof of the dilapidated Majumdar mansion to meet Mataji. We walked with Gandhiji to Noakhali.[8] We established a relief camp for the refugees in Chittagong. A friendship committee assembled in Dhaka. We took great care to break no laws. In spite of this, the authorities were suspicious of us. Shubendu who was a professor in Dhaka was dismissed. Samarendu was refused a doctor's licence. Yogendu died while taking part in relief work after the floods. This has always been Bengal's destiny, children! Nature herself is violent in Bengal—the sea continually attacks the land and overcomes it, whirlwinds blow and the Padma floods over. Cholera and starvation rage over the land. You know that such disasters cannot be confronted in terms of community and religion.

My younger daughter, Laila, married a Muslim. We all lived together. Those were the days when we listened in delight to my little three-year-old granddaughter, Naseema, sing Tagore's "Sonar Bangla."[9] She was the child the soldiers snatched away, dashed to the ground, and killed.

It is all over children! All, all over. All that was left to me at the end was the soil that was both mother and daughter to me, the soil on which I was born, my Bengal, with its turbulent rivers and lakes, its restless people. But that too is lost to me now.

Mujibur Sahib[10] once said to me, "Shanti Devi, you are the reflection of Bengal! You are mother and grandmother. Bless Bengal, that it may be free once more."

I had very little blood left in my body. Still, I cut my index finger and placed a *thilakam* on his forehead. "You must triumph, my son! Return victorious! May you succeed in making Bengal free!"

The freedom fighters who were Shanti Muthassi's grandchildren lifted her up and fled, and brought her to India. They call her a refugee here, a supplicant! A foreigner! Tell me, Indira,[11] is it true, has Shanti Majumdar come here as a refugee?

Is the mother of Dhiren, Samaren, Satyen, and Nityen a foreigner on this soil?

I, who am in the land of Tagore, of Sarat Chandra,[12] of C. R. Das, of Netaji, I ask you this: does Shanti Majumdar belong here, or is she a foreigner? If you say this is not my country. I do not want to die here. Oh, my tears flow again, my head reels. No, I will not weep. Dhirendu Majumdar's mother will not weep. Come, let us sing the song we used to sing then, long ago,

"You who wield sharp swords in your many hands!
You of the sweet fruit, clear water,
You, green and fertile,
Mataram, Vande Mataram . . . "

1973

NOTES

1. The story is set in 1971. When the people of East Pakistan fought for their independence from Pakistan, Bangladesh was established.
2. Nationalist leader who believed in achieving independence through an armed struggle. A schoolteacher by profession (therefore known as "Masterda"), he inspired many youths to join him in underground activities. He is best known for the Chittagong Armory Raid of 1930. He was hanged in 1934.
3. This daring terrorist attack by Surya Sen and his followers in 1930 succeeded in paralysing the state, even if temporarily.
4. Patriotic song composed by the Bengali litterateur Bankim Chandra Chattopadhyay in 1858. This is a translation of Lalithambika's Malayalam rendering of the song.
5. Tarakeshwar Dastidar (?–1934), Kalpana Dutta (1913–1995), Preetilata Wadeddar (1911–1932), Ganesh Ghosh (unknown), Savitri Roy (unknown) were all Masterda's followers.
6. Gopinath Saha attempted to shoot the notorious British official Tegart in 1924 but mistakenly killed another man (Day). When his trial was on, Gandhiji refused to plead on his behalf because, as the preacher of "ahimsa," he could not condone such acts of violence even if the motive was patriotic.
7. Trailokya Chakraborty was associated with revolutionary nationalist activities since his school days and was exiled to the Andamans. Later he worked with leaders like C. R. Das and Subhash Bose (Netaji)—

both mentioned at the close of the story. Nehru is Jawaharlal Nehru, the first Indian Prime Minister.

8. Riots broke out between the Hindus and Muslims in 1946. Noakhali in East Bengal was one of the worst affected places. After the large-scale violence Gandhi went on a pacifist mission to Noakhali.

9. *Amar Sonar Bangla, Ami Tomai Balobashi* ("Golden motherland Bengal, I love you"), Tagore's patriotic song which is now the national anthem of Bangladesh.

10. Sheikh Mujibur Rahman was the leader of the Bangladesh Liberation War; he became the first Prime Minister of independent Bangladesh. He was assassinated in 1975.

11. Indira Gandhi, the Indian Prime Minister during the Bangladesh War.

12. Bengali poet Rabindranath Tagore; Bengali novelist Sarat Chandra Chattopadhyay.

PART II

Memoir

⚜ Childhood Memories

BALYASMRITI   15

A VALLEY SURROUNDED by a fortress of hills, all the level ground divided into rice fields, the canal waters foam and whirl against the rocks, and sometimes they snake swiftly down. The hillsides where the cattle graze are filled with country flowers. There are rabbits and mountain squirrels everywhere. The Komaran Rock, which can be seen from every point around, towers over the landscape. Under it is a tiger's lair. Often we saw hunters with a tiger they had shot and hung on a pole, exhibiting it at the Devi temple in the village to the accompaniment of cries and ululations.

Anyone who wanted to get to the village had to walk through nearly four miles of field and hillside. An aristocratic wealthy *tarawad*, full of innumerable members of a vast extended family, stood in the centre of the village. Around it were the houses of the laborers, some of whom were of the upper castes, though most were untouchables or harijans. Many of the villagers were agricultural workers. There were separate communities of washerfolk, carpenters, and blacksmiths.

A little girl was born one morning sixty years ago in this big house that stood isolated from the outside world in the midst of hills. It was the Malayalam year 1084 (A.D. 1909), the month of Meenam, Friday the thirteenth. The star was Karthika.

Although her society considered it a curse to be born a girl, she was not wholly unwelcome. For one thing, her parents had lost two children and were longing for a baby. For another, she was born at the time when her grandfather, whose star was the same as hers, was praying to the Devi, chanting the "Lalitha Sahasranamam," the thousand names of the Goddess. And that is how she received her name, Lalithambika, which according to tradition should have been a different one.

Another anecdote that was always told to her along with this one, and was also to do with her birth, affected her very deeply over the years. When her father, a learned man of progressive views, heard that a daughter had been born to him, he exclaimed angrily, "No, I will not live here any longer. I'll go away, maybe to Madras, become a Christian, and marry an Englishwoman."

"And what if she has a daughter too?" asked my mother.

"At least I will be allowed to bring her up like a human being. I will have the liberty to educate her, give her the freedom to grow, get her married to a good man."

She had heard this story many times. Her eighty-year-old mother had repeated it to her just a few days ago. She had not understood its significance at first. Her father took great care not to let her realize that she had been born into a society that did not believe in bringing up girls as human beings. Her mother, who was her first teacher, began to instruct her at a very early age. Her *vidyarambham* ceremony was conducted when she was three years old. She would tug at her mother's *mundu* and take her away to her books until she learned to read herself. After that she began to read on her own: anything she could lay hands on, newspapers, magazines, books. She read indiscriminately, unceasingly.

CHILDHOOD
ENTE KUTTIKKALAM

My very first memory of early childhood is of the sounds I used to hear when I woke up in the morning: the chime of holy bells blending with the chants. I usually lay in bed for some time and listened. When I rose and came out, the *nalukettu* was always enveloped in the smoke of the Ganapathi *homam*. The fragrance of tulasi and sandalwood and of foods prepared for the *naivedyam* would waft out of the thevarappura.[1]

Amma rose very early in the mornings. She would have had a bath and begun the rituals of worship and the preparations for breakfast by the time I awoke. Many of the children would have had their baths. Because it was such a huge extended family, there was a certain lack of order in the routine of the household. But none of us were allowed to have breakfast till we had had a bath and said our prayers. I usually ran to the tank on the eastern side of the house, had a dip in it, dried myself rapidly, and rushed back. As a child of five or six, all I wore was a *konam* made of the spathe of a palm leaf or of red cloth. I first went to the temple, then worshipped all the household deities and prostrated before them. After this, I ate my share of the offerings: the milky sweet made for the worship that day, malar,[2] *trimadhuram*, and slivers of coconut. Then came breakfast, for which I had hot *kanji* with ghee and roasted pappadams.

In the mornings we had lessons with a teacher. All we took to class were a quill pen and a few sheets of paper. Pens with nibs were not very common in those days. We wrote with sharpened ostrich feathers, and made our own ink. We pounded kadukka nuts, mixed copper sulphate into it, added water, and left it in the sun in a frying pan. Sometimes we put in hibiscus flowers to improve the consistency. When the mixture had been sunned for four or five days and grown thick, we strained it and stored it in bottles.

We sat on the floor and wrote on little low desks, which had drawers in them to hold pens and ink. Writing in copybooks was a strict requirement. We began with a lesson in Sanskrit. After that we studied the government textbooks of the period. They were chosen for us according to the class we were suited for. We did arithmetic, geography, and history. In the afternoon, we were free for an hour and started lessons again after lunch only at three. We continued until the sun set. The music teacher came occasionally, in the morning or the evening.

At dusk, we said our prayers again. Achan sat with us after dinner, while we read the Puranams. All this left me very little free time. However, we managed to escape the watchful eyes of the grown-ups to run away and paddle and swim in the tanks, roam through the banana groves, and pick flowers. Wild rabbits played amongst the bushes. You could stand on the hill and watch the lovely sunsets and the green fields lying around. I have breathed the beauty of this landscape so often as a child.

There is a high school building on the hill now, and children instead of rabbits play on the hillside. Roads run all over and cars and buses go down them ceaselessly. Cement structures have been erected everywhere. I watch the children of the new generation and think that the human race has certainly made great progress, but is losing touch with nature. Is this a part of progress? Who are the fortunate ones, they or we? But then concepts like good fortune and happiness are relative after all.

THE BEGINNING
EZHUTHINTE ARAMBHAM

There were three portraits in the front room of their guesthouse. The first was of Swami Vivekananda delivering the Chicago address [in 1894]. The next one was of Gandhiji in a big turban, with a shawl around his shoulders. The third was a beautiful painting of Tagore, with eyes as wide as lotus petals, a long beard, and a loose robe. Her father's brother had brought the last two from Madras where he was a student. Discussions on the ideals and activities of the three persons in these portraits—on religion, nationalism, and literature—took place very often in the room where they hung. All three attracted her, but Gandhiji exerted the strongest influence over her. She began to think and write about him, and about the freedom of India. She tore up most of what she had written, but one or two articles were published.

Disturbing news filled the newspapers: the Mapilla Rebellion,[3] the satyagraha at Vaikkam,[4] the protest against land taxes. I recall the little girl engrossed in K. P. Kesava Menon's biography of Mahatma Gandhi,[5] bent almost double on the ground. She cried because she wanted to wear khadar. She bought a spinning wheel. She planted cotton and spun yarn. She put up pictures of the nationalist leaders on the walls of her room.

When she insisted she would wear nothing but khadar, her father asked, "What is so special about khadar?"

"It is a *swadeshi* product. Gandhiji has asked all of us to wear it."

Her father replied, "What about the mundus woven here, in Veliyath and Talachara? Aren't they swadeshi as well? Don't the weavers who make them have to make a living too?"

He was right. Her family always used mundus woven in the rural areas. She thought of the old weaver from Veliyath who usually brought them. His family lived on the paddy he received in exchange for the mundus.

She now perceives that most people who advocated khadar at the time were not truly interested in the ideals that inspired its manufacture, they wore it merely because it was in fashion. Around this time her father bought her a copy of Tagore's *At Home and Outside*.[6]

THE TREASURES OF MEMORY
ORMAYILE NIDHIKAL

She hardly ever left the protective circle of her fortress home, except for an occasional visit to her uncle's house, or, more rarely, to the house of a relative. Such expeditions had to be made in stages. First, there was a tiring walk of three or four miles, and then a journey of nearly four days, partly in a closely covered bullock cart and partly in a country boat.

Her father could be described as a child of the mountains, while her mother must have been the offspring of a water goddess, for she loved water. As a little girl she often saw crocodiles as their boat glided slowly over the Pamba River. Red and white water lilies grew in the fields and lotuses bloomed in profusion in the channels between them. The sand lay knee-deep in summer, and during the monsoon water flowed everywhere, as far as the eye could reach.

Boat rides with her uncle, festivals in the temple, a grandmother who adored her: all these filled her life with novelty and happiness.

As a child she did not think of herself as different from others, and it was only much later that she noticed that the quality that set her apart had certain disadvantages. As if in response to her father's wish, her mother bore no more daughters. She grew up with her brothers for company, learned whatever they did, and behaved no differently from them. Wooden kuradus[7] were not inserted in her earlobes to lengthen them in the customary manner and she never went bare-breasted. As she grew older, she was aware that people disapproved of the way she was being brought up. They thought that a growing girl had no right to so much freedom.

When she looks back now, she understands the meaning of the expression in her father's eyes every time she lingered in the room where literary discussions took place. He obviously could not bear to tell her to go to the inner rooms, to explain to her that she could no longer be with them now that she was growing up.

A CAGED BIRD
KOOTILE KILI

The event that her parents had dreaded took place at last. The day she reached puberty, the house looked and felt as if someone had died. Her mother wept, so did the rest of the family, and the servant women, and seeing them, she too could not help crying. Even her father, usually confident and assured, lamented: "I feel as if I have to cage a free bird."

She was like one dead now, as far as the outside world was concerned. She might not go to the temple, or play under the champakam tree. She might not talk to her favorite swami. She felt the impact of these changes very sharply over the next four days, and began to understand why her father had been so distressed when a daughter had been born to him.

Like everyone else around her, she had to submit to customs that had been observed strictly over many centuries. She knew that no concessions would be made for her, and that she had to bow to the dictates of destiny, no matter how deeply it hurt.

I feel that her real education took place during those two years, when she was confined to the *antahpuram*. She read a great deal during this period and wrote a little too. She reflected deeply and compassionately on the contradictions, the joys, and the sorrows, the ideals, desires, and experiences of all the people around her:

her immediate and extended family, her society and the laborers in the village. The longer she thought about them, the more intensely she shared their joys and sorrows. She often asked herself, "What if I were in their place?"

Three of her grandfather's sisters, who were child widows, lived with them and she observed them closely. She had heard the story of yet another sister who had been unjustly cast out when she was fifty years old for the crime of having gone out of the house without her umbrella in the midst of a family quarrel.[8] She had taken ill and died untended by the roadside.

Two or three young girls distantly related to her had been sold to people who came from north Kerala, on the pretext of being given in marriage. Nothing had been heard of them since.

She often thought that the souls of these unfortunate women inhabited her. What if I had been one of them, she would ask herself.

She wrote a novel in the narrative style of *At Home and Outside*. Poems, plays, and stories followed swiftly. She read them over and over again, cried over them, then tore them up.

She had no companions of her age at all.

MARRIAGE

VIVAHAM

Her parents became increasingly busy with their domestic responsibilities. Her brothers had left home to go to the English school about seven miles away from their village, and now lived in the vicinity of the school. Once she finished her household duties, she read, wrote, and watched the happenings in and around the house through the doors of the *nalukettu*. She never regretted those two years of solitude, which gave her the opportunity to nurture her inner vision and to define her ideals.

Discussions that would eventually decide their daughter's future must have taken place during this period, in the outer rooms and the kitchen of the big house. And that was how a good-looking, gentle, affectionate young man came into her life one day, like a messenger from the gods. He held her hand over the glowing flames of the sacrificial fire and said to her, "I take your hand in the certainty that it will bring good fortune to both of us. Will you follow me?"

She said yes silently in her heart. The priest said to them, "Your lives are now joined."

They have been mutually supportive companions now for forty-two years. There have been occasions when they felt too tired to go on, when they were lost and confused. But their griefs and burdens brought them closer together. When the dreamlike responses of the imaginative vision and the practical good sense of everyday reality go hand in hand, a new lineage is born.

Now that she had a comrade to help her achieve her aims and desires, she grew stronger. Her mind, free of its fetters, longed for complete freedom. It was a period when a group of young revolutionaries were actively engaged in trying to change society. They convened meetings, performed plays, and spoke on public platforms. Her village took part in these activities and organized public speeches and propaganda marches.

People began to see that art could be used as a powerful weapon. The waves of this impassioned social and national struggle swept through the darkest corners of the inner rooms and roused them into a new awareness of freedom.

WE CAST AWAY OUR UMBRELLAS
MARAKKUDA NEENGUNNU

She remembers it perfectly, the day they decided to hold that important meeting in a nearby town. A group of courageous women who had decided to cast away their umbrellas were going to be there. She pretended she was going to a temple, started out with her umbrella and shawl, and threw the umbrella away as soon as she left the house. She then rearranged the mundu that covered her as a saree, and took a bus to the venue of the meeting.

It gives her great pleasure now to think of that inspiring event. Bur she came back that day to find her mother in tears, sorrowing as if her daughter had died. Her relatives wanted nothing to do with her, and even the servants avoided her. Senior members of the family declared that they could not perform a *shraddha* in a house where a woman had been cast out. Others counseled that she be forbidden to enter the kitchen. It began to look as if the matter might lead to a legal dispute, or even partition of the family property. However, her father remained unruffled. "All right," he said, "she and her husband went to a public meeting together. Is that sufficient reason to cast her out? People have done worse things and not been so severely punished." He refused to be intimidated. And society gradually changed its norms.

I believe that each era evolves its own ideas and goals, and that they also depend on how old one is, the stage of life one has reached. It is the combination of these factors that compels human beings to action. The young woman therefore surrendered to her destiny, which was to express the thoughts and feelings within her. But when she began to put them down in writing, she did not ever think that she might someday become well known in the literary world. A friend came across some of the pieces she had written in her notebook and insisted that she send them to one of the leading Malayalam weeklies, which published them. The editor then asked her for a poem. She gave them a poem and a story. And so it all began . . .

She was determined to fulfill her literary and domestic duties, as well as her commitments to society, with an equal degree of dedication. They were all integral parts of her life and she could not bear to neglect any of them. She did not realize at the time that this obstinacy would result in her being unable to accomplish any of her tasks completely.

Meanwhile, there were babies every year. She brought them up. She wrote, read, and made speeches. When I look back, I see the young mother crouched on the ground, writing as she rocks the cradle. I see the willful, ignorant young woman standing on a public platform, holding her baby close to her while she makes a speech—the impudent woman who opposed anyone who did not agree with her, who used her art as a weapon against her adversaries, who stoically accepted the blows and wounds that her enemies in the literary world aimed at her.

She dealt with the world around her solely on the basis of information gleaned from the newspapers, and her vision of life was directed purely by her imagination. She saw the world in the light of her own beliefs—beliefs that changed constantly with the changing pace of the times. Only much later did she see that even the great men of the twentieth century could do little to alter the corrupt nature of the prevalent goals and methods of action, and that truth and justice had no place in political conflict.

Those who use the pen as a weapon often lacerate their own hearts with its needle-sharp point. She became sensitive to criticism and found herself wondering whether readers would be annoyed with her, whether they would misunderstand her. She tormented herself endlessly with self-censure.

But she persisted in her chosen way of action with extraordinary self-confidence, even at the risk of being considered insolent. Human beings are an assortment of defects, misdeeds, and contradictions that they wish upon themselves. Their definitions of defects and misdeeds vary according to the period they live in, the beliefs that guide them, and the circumstances in which they are placed. Who knows what is right and what is wrong? There are religions that believe that all men and women are born sinners. How innocently, how trustingly, they call themselves sinners! I am not prepared to go that far. But I do know that we often bruise and slash each other in order to achieve what we consider good. But who can tell whether what we thus achieve is truly good and right? Sometimes when we try to eliminate what we believe is bad in us, we lose an essential part of our individuality. What we thought of as a defect might well have been our strongest point.

As time went by, her impudence and her outspokenness were repeatedly crushed, and she had perforce to learn humility. With that, however, the artistic skills she had acquired began to weaken.

1969

NOTES

1. The room where the deities are kept.
2. Fried paddy.
3. See Introduction, p.xviii.
4. Nonviolent protest movement, 1924–1925, demanding the right of all castes to enter the Vaikkam temple; Gandhi was a participant.
5. K. P. Kesava Menon (1886–1973) was a well-known freedom fighter. He founded the Malayalam daily *Matrubhumi* in 1923. He was the author of many biographies and also translated Gandhi's *My Experiments with Truth* into Malayalam.
6. See Introduction, p.xix.
7. These were pieces of wood that were inserted into the pierced earlobes of the anterjanams to lengthen them. Gold ornaments called chittus could be worn only when the earlobes were long enough.
8. See Introduction, p.xxii.

A Writer Is Born

EZHUTHINTE EETTILLAM   16

WHO KNOWS with certainty what direction our lives may take at a given moment! The most insignificant incident, something we had never dreamed of, an unexpected word or look or act, may formulate a whole new pattern of life, whereas deliberate planning may be totally ineffectual. This unknown factor often influences the advance and retreat of the individual, of society, and the nation. I do not wish to call this factor fate. What is it then? I do not know. Who knows? I only know that it is the power that made me a writer of some repute, and also a social worker, when I could have remained an ordinary mother and housewife, confined to the kitchen.

The rejection of ghosha, the system of seclusion, for women was not a sufficiently important gesture in itself. It was an event that had become inevitable with the passage of time, that was a natural consequence of the establishment of a forceful social movement. The wearing of modern clothes achieved nothing in itself either. Once again, it was an instance of necessity becoming inevitable, and the forerunner of the actual abandonment of ghosha.

How and when did I then acquire this firm sense of vocation? An innate gift for literary creation could have limited itself, as M. P. Paul[1] once said, to the composition of a handful of devotional verses or hymns to Kali, had time and circumstance not favored its development in a wider sphere. What a writer, man or woman, needs most is freedom, the freedom to break family bonds and the courage to defy opposition of any kind. My husband gave me both. My parents did not actively oppose my inclination for literature; neither did they encourage it. They could not do much else, since they were heads of a family that was very deeply rooted in tradition. My father bought me excellent books, and my mother made me read them. I sent the little bits and pieces I wrote to women's magazines without letting my parents know. My life could well have continued on these lines forever.

At this juncture, namboodiri society was revitalized by the impulse towards a renaissance. Numerous associations and newspapers were established. The younger generation became very active under the leadership of V. T. Bhattadiripad[2] and performed his play, *From the Kitchen to the Scene of Action*. They realized that true social progress could not be achieved unless women were granted freedom, and efforts were initiated in this direction. The winds of a momentous change swept through the whole of namboodiri society. This is the article I contributed at the time to the jubilee souvenir of the Nair Service Society:

> I can think of so many incidents that illustrate Sri Mannath Padmanabhan's courageous ideals,[3] his far-sightedness and his fellow feeling for sister societies. I am proud to say that it was one of these very incidents that completely changed the direction of my very ordinary life. The children of today cannot even imagine the state of our society fifty years ago. It was a period when tradition dominated life; when the king administered the state, and when human beings believed that touch could pollute. Each caste had its own subcastes and every little group had its own rigid codes of behavior. These codes were so strictly imposed that the community had the right to cast an individual out for the most trivial lapse. Human beings were therefore enslaved not only politically but also by these traditions.
>
> The namboodiris are regarded as the highest caste

in Kerala. But namboodiri women suffered terrible miseries in the name of caste. Denied a modern education, once they reached puberty, they were incarcerated in the *antahpuram*, kept half-naked, with their breasts exposed, and had to live as asuryampasyakal, that is, those who were never allowed to look at the sunlight. If they went out, they had to screen their faces with a palm-leaf umbrella, cover themselves entirely with a shawl, and be accompanied by a chaperone. The only male face an *anterjanam* could ever look at was her husband's. Anterjanams were accused of the most inconsequential misdoings, for which they were tried by a smartavicharam[4] and then cast out of society. Fear was the only emotion they knew. The tears, the pain, and the suffering of unhappy anterjanams, old spinsters, widows disowned by their families and dissatisfied co-wives, filled the antahpurams, which were worse than Hitler's concentration camps.

A group of young men with progressive views founded the Yuvajana Sangham around this time. They saw that they would never know true freedom as long as one half of society was plunged in suffering and the darkness of ignorance. They diffused their propaganda through the stories and poems they wrote and the plays they performed. It is said that spectators belonging to other communities were moved to tears when they saw the hardships of namboodiri women realistically depicted in plays like V. T. Bhattadiripad's *From the Kitchen to the Scene of Action*, and M. R. Bhattadiripad's *The Hell Beneath the Screen of the Umbrella.*[5] Meanwhile, the orthodox were infuriated when they saw an anterjanam without her umbrella and shawl, even on the stage.

These movements in the outside world found their echoes in the antahpurams: their inhabitants began to wonder whether play-acting could not, indeed, be transformed into reality. As a result, seven young anterjanams, with Parvathi Nenmini Mangalam and Arya Pallam at their head, walked into the Yuvajana Sangham assembled in Trittala. It was an unprecedented gesture and people were shocked. Many thought the anterjanams were men dressed as women, as in the plays of the time. The general reaction was to accuse the women of being impudent and willful. I would like to record, however, with deep gratitude, that Mannath Padmanabhan was the very first person to welcome and felicitate the young women. It was his acceptance of their gesture that gave me too my freedom. I do not know if history books have documented this event, but it still glows radiantly in my memory.

The year was 1107 (A.D. 1932), the month Meenam, the day the sixteenth or the seventeenth. On the occasion of the Nair Sammelanam at Mavelikkara, Mannath Padmanabhan decided to hold a reception to honor Nenmini Mangalam and Arya Pallam, the anterjanams who had abandoned ghosha. This was announced in the papers and all of us who were members of the anterjanams' associations in mid-Travancore were inexpressibly happy to hear the news. The legal resolution to do away with ghosha had been passed, but none of us had actually adopted it in practice. Nor did we believe that we would ever be able to go out without our umbrellas and shawls. We all had limitations to contend with: the tyranny of family relationships, opposition from orthodox members of the community, a constant fear of being cast out of society and, of course, a cowardly reluctance to break with long established customs. But here were two young women come to show us the way to freedom, like messengers from the gods, and here was a great leader who had raised his hand in blessing to them—and, through them—to us. If I did not go now to join them, whispered my heart, I would never go. I decided to attend the meeting in Mavelikkara, regardless of the consequences. I left the house that day on the pretext of going to worship at a temple nearby. I threw away my umbrella as soon as I reached the bus stand. I had already worn a saree instead of covering myself with the usual enveloping *mundu*. When I arrived at the venue of the meeting, with the respected president of our association, Devi Parvathi Anterjanam (she was Sastri Damodaran's mother, and died recently at the age of a hundred years) and the secretary, Devaki Kainikkara (who later became a member of the Travancore

Assembly) and a few other anterjanams, the function had already started. Mannath knew most of our families. I had met
him when I was a little girl, when I had accompanied my
parents on the occasion of the founding of the Kuruvatta High
School. He had held my hands and counseled me never to
wear bell metal bangles, since they would be sure to grow
green with tarnish. He was visibly surprised to see me, and
welcomed me warmly: "I never thought you would come. I
am so happy. It is a great victory for us. Please sit with all
the distinguished guests."

Kottur Bhagirathi Amma presided that day. The *pandal*
was packed with people who had come to see the anterjanams. Pointing to the celebrities on the dais and to us, Mannath Padmanabhan made a witty speech: "What you see here
now is not an illusion. All these women are anterjanams who
have shed their stigma. Close your eyes, those of you who
are afraid that you will go blind if you look at anterjanams!"

I am proud to have been one of that gathering. The rejection of seclusion, the revocation of the laws of pollution, the
modernization of customs: none of these may seem over-
whelmingly important matters now. Four decades ago, however, they were events of major significance.

When we returned from the meeting at Mavelikkara, I
found my family in turmoil. Achan smiled gravely. Amma
wept, beat her head, and lamented, "I wish I had never had
a daughter. If only she had died as soon as she was born. I
do not want a daughter like you . . . " I knew her grief was
sincere, but it did not move me at all. The more orthodox
members of the family—indeed, even my father's brothers,
who considered themselves comparatively progressive—received us coldly. They refused to perform my grandfather's
shraddha along with Achan, because I was present in the
house, and stormed out angrily. They would not take part in
the religious rites. It was much worse in my husband's household, where there were old uncles and grandmothers who
were rigid disciplinarians. I was very distressed and did not
know what to do. My husband had not completed his educa-

tion and did not have a job. He and I gave the matter much thought. Finally we told Achan that we would rent a small house and move into it, so that there would be peace at home. Achan's eyes filled with tears. After a long silence, he said: "Don't rush into anything. Have patience. I'll find a way—"

Achan bought a bit of land at some distance from the *illam* and built us a little house on it. We called it "Bhaskara Vilasam." Paddy fields surrounded it and hills lay beyond them. The rays of the rising sun fell straight into the front veranda. We moved into this beautiful home with our small children. We had nothing to fear now. Caste discrimination did not exist in this place, and innumerable people visited us, regardless of caste or creed—our own friends, and my brothers' friends. My husband cultivated the land. We spun yarn and wove mundus on our own loom. We even presented Gandhiji with two mundus we had woven when he came to visit that area. The garden I had dreamed about for many years blossomed around our house and in my heart.

I read a great deal. I wrote stories and poems. I sent them to leading magazines and they were accepted for publication. Well-known persons like C. V. Kunhiraman[6] visited us. We breathed and experienced freedom every minute of our lives. Eventually, I owned literature as much as it owned me.

One of our guests once wrote these lines on the wall of our home:

> "We live as brothers
> In this ideal place
> Where caste and creed
> Do not divide us."

For the next ten years, we lived a simple self-sufficient life, and followed Gandhiji's principles. Then Achan died, quite suddenly. Our children were growing up fast, and we now had to think of their education. I fell seriously ill. Our needs increased; we could no longer manage with a tiny bit of land as our sole possession. Moreover, in namboodiri society, a married daughter has no place in her father's house. In the end, much against my will, we had to move to my husband's house, with its innumerable inmates, its endless domestic squabbles, and its old-fashioned ways of living. Meanwhile we had learned to use our tools skillfully: my husband his hoe, and I my pen.

"Bhaskara Vilasam," which gave us our identity, now belongs to strangers. But the literary vocation I carved out there continues to flourish. The inner spaces of my heart still glow bright with the radiance of that time, and the flowers that bloomed then have not faded. I have not sacrificed my ideals. As I sit in the twilight of the present and think of the bright mornings in "Bhaskara Vilasam," I know with absolute clarity that what art needs most of all for its development is freedom. What would become of us if we did not have a home of our own, if we never knew affection and friendship?

1967

NOTES

1. A writer and critic, especially of the short story and the novel.
2. See Introduction, p.xix.
3. Founder of the Nair Service Society (NSS) in 1914 on the model of the Servants of India Society that had been set up by G. K. Gokhale; he was an active social reformer.
4. See Introduction, p.xxii.
5. See Introduction, p.xix–xx, for details on the plays.
6. He started the *Kerala Kaumudi* in 1911; he worked hard to spread the teachings of Sree Narayana Guru, the ezhava leader.

A Woman Writer's Reply

KATHAKARTHRIYUTE MARUPATI   17

IT IS AN ardent interest in life that compels life to reveal itself.[1] Well-wrought and powerful artistic creations can only take shape from an overwhelming love for life. The inner spirit absorbs the transient perceptions gleaned by the five senses and turns them into experience. Literature takes its stimulus from a background of dreams, where the truth of reality merges with the fanciful colors of the imagination. This phenomenon can perhaps be compared to the way in which the radiance of the sun touches the surface of the moon and turns into moonlight. The dream vision sees the world with greater beauty than that of reality. Although a seed sprouts in the earth, it grows into the sky, spreads there, and bears fruit. The seeds of art are like this—only if they germinate in the imagination and grow into reality can they become true creations of art.

When I first began to write, I wrote poetry. Poetry is a wave of emotion that overflows into the mind, or a spark of feeling that kindles a blaze there. The beauty of narration and the weight of thought have no part in it. If poetry cannot contain everything one wants to say, other modes of expression evolve naturally. This is how I became a writer of short stories. The short story is the art form best suited to the powerful interpretation of a comprehensive

union of thought and emotion, especially for those who are determined to achieve a definite aim in the course of their service to
art. This must be why many writers have shifted from the medium
of the poem to that of the short story.

Surprisingly, my first work of art was a novel. I must have been
fifteen or sixteen when I wrote it. I had just read Tagore's *At Home
and Outside*,[2] translated into Malayalam by B. Kalyani Amma. The
book attracted me deeply. I read it many times. I felt that Vimala,
Sandipan, and the widowed sister-in-law were all part of my family.
I loved to relate the stories and novels I read to my companions,
most of whom were not literate. But I found that this was not a
story I could easily narrate, and it therefore lived within me. I appreciated its technique very much.

An anterjanam who was distantly related to us and who had no
means of her own, lived with us. She often talked to me, and told
me many stories of her sad life. She had two children and had
been abandoned by her husband. The destitute woman grieved
more over the sorrows of other people than her own. She always
lamented the fate of her younger sister, who had left home many
years before. "She was the seventh girl in the family," she said,
"and like a gift from the gods. She had lovely long hair and a won-
derfully fair skin. That was why—" She wiped away her tears and
went on with the story. They were very poor, and their father was
dead. They despaired of being able to give the young girl a dowry.
Marriage brokers who heard of the girl got in touch with them
and told them about a man who did not want a dowry and who
was even willing to pay a bride-price. He belonged to the em-
brandiri caste and came from north Kerala. They hinted that he
might be a little too old for the girl, but that this did not matter.
The man was wealthy and would take care of his wife.

Their older brother obviously rationalized thus. How would he
find a young and handsome bridegroom for a girl who had no
money? This seemed a good solution to the problem. They did not
have to spend any money, and the girl would be well settled. If
she was destined to be happy, all would go well with her. He pro-
ceeded with the arrangements for the marriage.

They did not know the name of the bridegroom's family or of

his village. The young girl could not even follow the language he spoke. When the fourteen-year-old girl was told to go with her fat old husband, she clung to her mother and sobbed loudly. "Amme, I'm afraid—" Mother and daughter wept. The brother dragged the young girl away from her mother and forced her to go with her husband. Thirty years had passed and they had never seen her again. They did not know whether she was alive or dead.

The story distressed me greatly. It was not fiction or hearsay, and I thought that if I had been born in a family like hers, the same thing could have happened to me. Her frightened cry, "Amme, I'm afraid—" and the thought of her large eyes, filled with tears, haunted my imagination. I felt that I had to give the story expression. Its details merged into those of *At Home and Outside*, and I decided to write a novel. It was about Devaki, a young girl, a dikshitar,[3] and Mallinathan, a young man. The dikshitar takes Devaki away and sells her to prostitutes. A young Bengali, Mallinathan (who is visiting a brothel for the first time) rescues her and takes her home with him. And so it goes on—I don't remember the story fully. No one except me ever saw the novel. It lay in an old box for years and was finally devoured by white ants. All the same, it was my first story.

My first publication was a short story called "The End of a Journey," in the illustrated weekly, *Malayala Rajyam*. It was a free rendering of a story by Sitadevi Chattopadhyay that had appeared in the *Modern Review*.[4]

Tagore was my god in the early phase of my literary career. I read his works in the translations done by Puthezhath Raman Menon and Kalyani Amma. Later, I read Bankimchandra and other Bengali novelists. The works of Sri Ramakrishna Paramahamsa and Swami Vivekananda, which I was encouraged to read when I was very young, helped me formulate my ideas and ideals. Even now, I feel that my imagination gropes in their shadow—or rather, their radiance.

If you ask me which of my stories I like the best, or which of my children I love the most, I cannot answer. Once I write a story, I do not read it again. Therefore, all I can say is that I like everything that appeals to all of you.

It is not always possible to relate a story to a particular incident. For the story sometimes moves from the realm of the unconscious to the conscious only after many days, or even years. When it begins to take a definite shape, it disturbs me, and I have to write. The warmth and fluidity of the original may have faded by this time. The imaginative reconstruction of an event may take away its freshness, but it certainly acquires new distinctive features and a ripeness, a mellowness of its own. The origin of a story does not subjugate a writer, rather, the writer remains in command and uses it assertively. This is not always possible. No one narrates a story exactly as it happened. It evolves its own shape and end. For example, when I intended a story to have a happy ending, it sometimes ended tragically. Sometimes, it happened the opposite way. As the characters move within the range of experience, a right and good ending evolves naturally.

What we call inspiration is the awakening of the creative impulse. There is a powerful stimulus behind every great story, a longing to give shape to the ideas that crowd turbulently into the mind. There are people who deny the existence of inspiration and who maintain that one can write without it. But unless one writes merely to get rid of some troublesome matter, the impulse of inspiration awakens every time one begins to write. I will not describe here the quality of the sweet restlessness that takes hold of the writer from the moment of inception of a narrative, through its development, until its appearance as a story that charms, for if this restlessness makes itself felt, it is not something that can be put in words.

Imagination reflects the likenesses and experiences of real life and turns them into art forms. They are not chosen deliberately, nor is it always clear in whom, how, and when they originated. Imagination uses what exists within oneself, although it often takes a complex form. Ideas are the most important element of romantic stories. When people with similar thought processes write, their work may manifest similar traits and even lay them open to a charge of plagiarism.

Amongst all the imaginary characters I have created, I particularly like the Punjabi girl in "A Leaf in the Whirlwind," because she is drawn completely from the imagination. I had not visited Punjab when I wrote the story, nor had I met any refugees. I read in the newspaper one day that a certain number of women who had been raped would be handed over at the border in exchange for the same number from this side. When I went to bed that night, I thought of this bit of news and the identity of one of the women refugees who had endured such unimaginable sorrow took shape in my mind. I got up at once and wrote the story. The image of this girl, who reflects the distress of one caught in a terrible dilemma of womanhood, is very dear to me, for it was my imagination that created her.

I have never tried to employ a particular technical mode for a story. Each story evolves the technique best suited to it. There must be different modes for the romantic story, the realistic story, and the pen portrait, and what is good for one may not succeed in another. I once tried to write a story based on the chain of experiences that the human race must have undergone at the time when it began. My intention was to write a series of such stories. But I felt that I did not have the scientific knowledge necessary for such a project and gave it up.

A good writer is never ignorant.

I do not wish to answer the eleventh question. Literature that is subservient to the demands of the times changes according to the mien of the period in which it is written (although the mien alone is not the soul). The literature of the atomic age will therefore have its own special qualities.

No one begins to write with an exclusively private vision of life. As writing progresses, however, such a vision is bound to take shape. The fiction writer's vision of life is evident all the way through the story.

Propaganda is not a writer's aim, but ideas, desires, and goals that the writer has evolved are often propagated through art. All good literature has this aspect, and even Valmiki and Vyasa wrote [their epics] in this medium.

Readers have now begun to prefer the novel to the short story. This may be because imagination and experience have grown so vast that they cannot be contained within the limits of the short story. I do not want to mention the names of the short story writers who have succeeded or failed in becoming novelists. They are still writing, and we are still reading, so it is too early to form opinions.

I believe that even as the artist, man or woman, pulls down the girders of a narrow, decayed society, he or she must also forge the tools to build a cultured and wholesome new structure in its place. All artistic creations—novels, short stories, and poems—are materials to be used for this purpose.

1962

NOTES

1. This article is undated, but most probably appeared in 1962 since it was written in response to a questionnaire by the Malayali poet G. Sankara Kurup in the journal *Tilakam*, October 1962. Lalithambika Antherjanam's article was also published by *Tilakam*.
2. See Introduction, p.xix.
3. A Tamil priest.
4. The younger daughter (1893–1974) of Ramananda Chattopadhyay, the influential editor of the *Modern Review* (founded 1901), she wrote essays and novels in Bengali.

Lessons from Experience

ORU KATHIKAYUDE

ANUBHAVAPADANGAL   18

DEAR READERS!

I know that this is an extremely outmoded way to start, but for the present I cannot do otherwise. The editors of *Malayalanadu* have decided to devote this year's Onam issue to articles by fiction writers, requesting us to contribute something in the way of advice. Alternatively, I can describe how I came to be a fiction writer. Both are difficult tasks. The first is something I cannot do. It is impossible for one person to advise another in the domain of art, and undesirable as well. Each generation discovers the path it wants to follow. Although the way to the future lies through the past, it has to be defined according to each one's individual needs. Advice from those who have gone ahead has no value in this area.

And then, if you ask how I became a writer, it is not easy to explain. Many people have asked me this and I have not been able to give an answer. Maybe I do not know the answer clearly myself. If you ask me why I was born a woman, what can I say? And what if you ask why I was born into this particular family, of these parents, at this point in time? Or why a passion for literature took hold of me in such an extraordinary fashion? These are all unanswerable questions.

People have often asked me why it is that hardly any women of the last generation in Kerala, or indeed in the whole world, dedicated themselves to the creation of literature. It has now been established that this was not because we lack talent or power of expression, but because of the way in which we were crushed by circumstances. It is often said that the women of Kerala (except those who belong to certain communities) enjoy the most freedom in India. But even in Kerala they are relegated to the category of scheduled castes and scheduled tribes as far as literature is concerned. They keep their distance from literature, as if an involvement with it may pollute them, make them untouchable. For women of highborn families may not allow their voices to be heard outside the home. They may, if they wish, dress elaborately or make themselves up to look beautiful. They may function as heroines of poems of obscure authorship or exult in being objects of passion. But, apart from a handful of devotional poems, we have not heard of anything written by them. Why?

Very long ago, one of the best loved poets of the Malayalam language asked me on a public platform: "Why has there not been a single woman poet in this land, where the Goddess of Poetry is conceived and worshipped in a woman's form? Although they are eulogized as personifications of passion, why has not even one of them composed a single line of love poetry?" He held up his chair, and demanded: "Look at this—this is a tool made of wood. It has four legs, a back, a seat. Has woman, after all, functioned only as a tool like this?"

I was distressed. I did not quite follow the comparison between a woman and a chair. Was womanhood an inanimate object like a block of wood, for others to chisel and carve? If a work of art had warmth and movement and the power to make decisions, what would it become? This poet had certainly written innumerable love poems, but if a young woman composed love poetry, did he understand what her life in society would become? Would he allow his sister to go in search of love, experience love, as he himself did?

Besides, from time immemorial, poets have with indulgence

called woman weak, deceitful, and cowardly. Because women have constantly heard this, they have come to believe it too. Eyes like black kuvala blossoms. Cheeks like roses. A forehead like the crescent moon. And lips like red tondi fruits. But no one looked at the heart trembling within that breast, its warmth and power, its tears and hopes.

Women, as conceived in literature, were always objects of pleasure. Even the shining models from history and the epics have lost their glow. According to Christian belief, the very first woman was, after all, accursed. Although it was on the evil advice of the serpent, it was she who plucked the fruit of the Tree of Knowledge and she who offered it to her husband. As for her husband, who attained knowledge, he realized the danger of allowing her to taste the fruit and deliberately snatched it from her. Thus she became a sinner in her husband's eyes as well as in the eyes of God. And so Eve, made from Adam's rib, plods on, shouldering the burden of her curse, the eternal representative of womanhood. As for the Hindu epics: Sita was repudiated, Draupadi was dishonored. In Rajput times, Meera had to take poison, Padmini had to jump into the fire. In the modern age, when tradition loosens its grip on them, they will show you. Wait and see. The very flow of your poetry will change direction—

I think I said something like that. When the meeting was over, the young poet asked me, "If you were to have the fruit of the Tree of Knowledge now, Chechi, what would you do with it?"

I laughed. "Don't you know? I'm a woman too, remember—like the very first woman, I too will put it into your mouth, younger brother."

This incident took place thirty-five years ago. The poet is now dead. But many of those present that day are still alive. And the women artists of the new generation now respond heatedly to many of the accusations leveled on that day. Although, in proportion to the total population, there are not as many women writers as there are men, there are still a considerable number. They are as proficient as men in the domain of the short story, the poem, the novel, and the critical review. This is an important example of the way in which the passage of time has transformed society. People like me, who began to write half a century ago, now belong to the old-fashioned group. And this is why I refuse to give the younger generation of fiction writers any advice.

However, if it will not bore you, I would like to relate an experience or two to you.

I think there has been the same sort of duality in my life that many women writers face: the conflict between the individual as an artist and the individual as a member of the family. A woman has to act both roles effectively. She has to be consistently sincere. For a man, the family is a refuge, a resting place. But it is the main area of action for a woman, and if she fails here, she fails totally. At the same time, the province of art demands the complete dedication of the soul. So she must read, study, think, write, and engage in debate. There is no room for narrow thoughts in this vast domain of activity.

I began to write within the constraints of family life. I tried to reconcile my two roles as best I could. I cooked and served. I nursed my babies. I fulfilled my duties as wife and mother. All this must certainly have weakened my position in the world of art, for I have never been able to write a poem or a novel or an article that demanded deep concentrated thought and experience, that monopolized my time and attention. Unhappily, I also had the impudence to take on the role of a social reformer. I reacted against what I could not accept through the art form and in those days, this was not as simple an activity to indulge in, like playing the veena or chanting poetry. If someone took note of what I wrote, a heated reply followed, to which I had to respond. Someone else would write a spirited rejoinder to this, and so it would go on, endlessly. Sometimes the reactions and responses took entirely unexpected turns.

Almost forty years ago, in 1934 or 1935, I wrote a story called "School Pranayam" in the *Malayala Rajyam*, an illustrated weekly published in Kollam. A schoolteacher falls in love with his student, a harijan girl. She becomes pregnant, and since she wants to save her teacher's reputation she leaves the village. After an interval of twenty years, we come upon a seamstress who lives in a village very far from the first one. Her daughter has an affair with a teacher in her school. The mother learns of it, goes in search of her daughter's seducer and finds her self face to face with her old teacher, the eternal lover. The mother gives him the child—not as a wife, but as his daughter (a childish plot! wouldn't you agree?). I can swear a thousand times over that this was an entirely imaginary story. But someone traced a resemblance to someone else, and wrote a story in reply. I received anonymous letters. The story called "The Power of Fate" had the same chain reaction. Around this time, I came across an article in the *Yogakshemam*, the mouthpiece of the Namboodiri Yogakshema Sabha, which carried the accusation that everything in that periodical supposedly written by *anterjanams* was really written by men, and that this kind of literature was thought "commendable." I wrote a story in reply, called it "Is this commendable?" and sent it to *Yogakshemam*. This too became a subject of hot debate. I was repeatedly counseled not to be provocative, not to place weapons deliberately in the hands of my adversaries, but I could never resist the urge to instigate a clash of ideas or theories.

There was a magazine called *Srimati*, published from Trivandrum, which claimed that it was run by women, and many important women were on the board of editors. I contributed to it regularly and with great enthusiasm. (Edapally Raghavan Pillai,[1] who died prematurely, edited the special issue.) Sadasyatilakam T. K. Velu Pillai[2] instituted an amendment of the current Nair Bill in the law courts, which allowed Nair men to resume the practice of marrying more than one wife. Belonging as I did to a society that suffered deeply from the ills of polygamy, I was profoundly shocked by this. I wrote a story called "Amends Made by an Amendment" and sent it to *Srimati*. Here too, needless to say, I attacked the principle and not the individual. But, most unexpectedly, an article by a V. G. Nair and a story in response to mine appeared in *Srimati*. Their main purport was: Why did a brahmin woman want to meddle in the affairs of the nairs? This hurt me. I entitled my reply, "A Caste Demon's Defence." The gist of it was that I considered that all women belonged to one caste, that of woman, and if I was wrong in my belief, any courageous nair woman could write openly to me. (I still have the article and the story, but this is not the time or place to include them.)

The editor asked to be forgiven and I felt vindicated. However, I learned later, from Sri Madasserry[3] that both the article and the story that had appeared in response to mine had been written by Sri E.V. Krishna Pillai, and that he had been more or less in the same circumstances as my hero. What an astonishing likeness imagination has to reality!

"Realism" again, is a story I wrote in a mischievous frame of mind for *Navajivan*, in order to illustrate a specific point. Once more, it led to a misunderstanding with a very dear friend, Thakazhi.[4]

Literature boasts of a famous heroine called Kuriyedathu Tatri,[4] who belonged to the namboodiri society and who was declared an outcaste by her community. I wrote a story called "The Goddess of Revenge" with hearsay material that I had pieced together. This was a period when anterjanams were forbidden to even pronounce Tatri's name. I received many anonymous letters. A man wrote, "If you believe that Tatri is a goddess, write verses to her. You are the only one who can do it."

Furious at the cruel mockery implied in this, I replied, "I do not know Tatri's story. Only men can tell it as it really happened: the sixty-four men who were witnesses to it. If you tell me the story, I will write it."

And so one story led to another. It was such a delight, in those days. My blood was hot, my mind inspired, and injustices that needed to be exposed lay everywhere around me.

I do not know whether art—pure art—can be used as a medium of propaganda. Since artists, men or women, are social animals, society's emotions, the experiences, and demands enter into their very being. They become part of a collective imagination and fashion new concepts. Even the maharishis, or sages of old, believed that "the welfare of all is the happiness of all." I think it is because they represent the consciousness of society that writers are able to simultaneously feel the emotions of the individual as well as the multitude. The poetic consciousness attains the magical power that releases each of us from the cage of the self and allows me to become you, you to become me. Art is not the composition of short articles. Art is a force that awakens all the powers of expression that are within the self and addresses them toward the entire universe. It is a mutual debate. It is also a mutual agreement. Which is why, readers, I addressed this article to you.

Think of it. What an insignificant woman I was—a village woman, confined to the *antahpuram*, ignorant of even the world she lived in. Illiterate, uneducated, and powerless. And yet, I could not resist taking up the cause of those who sighed and wept around me, whose sighs and tears eventually became a hurricane of protest here in Kerala, in Bharat, in the entire world. In time, those stormy voices learned to make music on even the slenderest bamboo stems. Clay idols woke and came alive. I too became a poet. And a writer of stories. And this is my story.

If the mode of bliss, which is the ideal of pure art, were my only medium, I would have spent my life, as M. P. Paul[5] once said, writing verses to Kali or *kaikottikkali* songs. I would not have had to walk through fire to find the power of expression. I would have transformed sorrows into joys. What use is it to say that now? Some people are made that way: they live in the sorrow of all living creatures, like Lord Vishnu does, and invoke that sorrow into themselves. An old friend asked me the other day, "Is sorrow still your preferred *rasa*?" What could I answer? Tears and flaming sparks were once my instruments. The sparks have grown cold. Can those lumps of coal be transmuted into stars? Can tears be enclosed in shells and changed into pearls? I do penance. As I meditate on the truth of the world, even grief becomes *prasadam*.

I do not wish to offer a single word of advice. New writers discover their own modes and write of what they see and experience. They are the heirs to the future. But other generations will follow them and make changes and new rules. And so it will go on till the wheel of rebirth ceases to turn. Since art is an indivisible component of human life, it will continue to progress in spite of change. When we look back at our heritage, however, it is important that we recognize a clump of forest trees, a bower, a cluster of mukutti flowers, as part of our past. Our times—our ways—must be made eternal through the creations of art. For it is art that has kept alive the true history of humankind.

I have read somewhere that Einstein said that we can understand the meaning of life only through continued dedication to society. Einstein was a great man of science. He wanted to find out how the great forces of the world operate and explain them to us. I think all artists, and indeed the entire human race, can profit from his advice. Even the sages taught a philosophy that diffused from the individual into the multitude.

Enough. Let me stop here. I know that literature is essential for the happiness of the soul as well. Old people love to talk to the younger generation. Forgive me, if I have spoken too much. Whatever we do, when we say, "the happiness of my soul," let us add, "is the welfare of all."

1972

NOTES

1. A poet (1909–1936), known for his romantic and lyrical poems that are full of a brooding melancholy.
2. "Sadasyatilakam" was the title given to this royal officer (1882–1950) for his magnificent work in updating the Travancore State Manual.
3. A Malayali writer (1910–1979) who wrote on Kunchan Nambiar, Vallathol, and Ulloor.
4. The novelist Thakazhi Sivasankara Pillai, born 1914.
5. A writer and critic, especially of the short story and the novel.

An Account of a Performance

ORU NADAKATHINTE KATHA   19

I T WAS ON A rainy day in the month of Mithunam in the year 1109
(A.D. 1934) that Sivaramakrishna Iyer, a teacher in the Kulakuda
special school, whom we knew well, came to our house to ask
me to write a play. The Kulakuda High School had been founded
not only to impart instruction in the Vedas to namboodiri children,
but also to give them a modern education. My brothers went to
this school, as my children were to later. The headmaster was the
well-known poet and literary figure, Subramanya Potti. The school
wanted to perform a play on the occasion of his retirement in Thu-
lam, and they had sent word to me to write one for them.

The request unnerved me. I had written a few stories for *Malayala Rajyam* and they had been appreciated by readers. But I had
never seen a play performed on the stage! I was not at all confident
that I could write one and was frightened of trying. I said that I
could not do it, but Sivaramakrishna Iyer was insistent. "Please
make an effort, I'm sure you can do it. After all, such knowledge
is not inborn, it is acquired by trial and experience."

In the end, I told them I would make an attempt. They wanted
the play by the month of Karkatakam. Sivaramakrishna Iyer said
he would arrange for rehearsals by then. I thought about the matter
all night and tried out many plots in my mind. I finally decided to

write a play on the remarriage of widows, which was not allowed at the time, nor did I expect that it would ever be. I had a few ideas and my enthusiasm grew as I wrote. When I had finished writing ten scenes, Sivaramakrishna Iyer came and took them away, and they began rehearsals.

In the month of Chingam, an amazing event took place. For the very first time in our society, a widow married again. V. T. Bhattadiripad[1] conducted the ceremony when M. R. Bhattadiripad[2] married a widow, Umadevi Anterjanam. Several members of our community extended their cooperation and gave their blessing. I felt extremely happy and sent a letter of good wishes to the couple.

Meanwhile, my play was ready, and was performed on the appointed day. The young boys who acted gave an excellent performance and the production was greatly appreciated. It was repeated at Kottarakkara, at the anniversary function of a library. In 1110 (A.D. 1935), in the month of Dhanu, the Yogakshema Sabha[3] wanted it performed at Haripad.

Although the resolution commending the remarriage of widows was turned down at the general body meeting of the Yogakshema Sabha, the Yuvajana Sangham[4] succeeded in their efforts to arrange for a gift to be given to the newly married couple. Vazhakunnam and Pariyanampatta were in charge. I gave them the ring I wore on my finger. Others gave watches, rings, and gold chains.

My play was to be performed at night. It dealt with the cruel pressures exerted by society on a young girl who was widowed on the third day of marriage, before she and her husband had even spent a night together. The talented boys of the special school acted the touching story with deep feeling.

When Kainikkara Kumara Pillai spoke after the performance, he said that those who had turned down the resolution that morning would certainly have accepted it if they had seen the play.

G. Ramachandran, the editor of *Chitravarika,* commented in the journal, "I saw the very people who had been against the remarriage of widows wipe away their tears when they saw the play, and heard them say that widows in such distressing situations should certainly marry again."

It must have been the harshness of the resolution forbidding

widows to remarry that made my play such a success. It was performed again next year at the meeting of the Yogakshema Sabha
in Thrissur, and another group in north Kerala asked for it. Although it was very widely appreciated and Kainikkara Kumara Pillai
offered to write the foreword himself, I never had the play published. A vague fear prevented me from doing so. I had called the play
"A New Birth," but the title was changed to "Savitrikutty" when it
was performed. I did not even have it printed. I did have the satisfaction that the play achieved what I had hoped it would, and that
its message had been fulfilled.

It seems to me now, when I look back, that many young widows
who belonged to our family must have been in my thoughts when
I wrote the play. The sad, innocent, unfortunate ghosts of these
women, who had suffered for sins that they had not committed,
haunted the plot. It must have been a reluctance to remove the
screen of the *anterjanam's* umbrella from their hidden faces that
held me back from having the play published. What atrocities I
had witnessed, and what terrible things I had heard about them!

Shantadevi Chattopadhyay's "The End of a Journey," written in
Bengali and translated by Sitadevi Chattopadhyay into English, appeared in the *Modern Review*.[5] Hearing the story read gave me the
idea for the first story I wrote for the *Chitravarika*, about a child
widow.

Some time before this, I had tried to render a story I had
heard into verse. I must have been fourteen or fifteen at the
time. When I met the subject of my poem, I had already heard
about her from Amma. She lived near my uncle's house. When
she was eighteen, an eighty-four-year-old namboodiri had married her, hoping to have children by her. He died three or four
months later. I saw her when she was about forty. She was still
extremely beautiful. She lived in an atmosphere of constant suspicion and slander. I was young and susceptible, and her circumstances inspired me to write. My composition flowed into a
number of verses, describing the young woman standing by the
bathing tank at dawn on the day before her wedding, and dedi-
cating her soul to the sun, and nature's compassionate response.
I quote a stanza from memory:

"Pale and thin with grief
The young bride wept.
The compassionate wind
Sighed to hear
The namboodiri child's
Sorrowing lament."

I saw another child widow when I once went on a visit with Amma. Namboodiri couples could spend a night together only on the fourth day of the wedding. This child had been married when she was twelve to a young man well suited to her in age and appearance. Bitten by a snake, he died on the third day of the wedding. The child cried bitterly when the *thali* thread around her neck was broken. According to tradition, she would not be considered free from pollution until the ceremony of "sekam," to celebrate the physical union of the young couple, had been performed. An image of her husband was therefore made from darbha grass and his spirit was invoked into it. This image was used to perform the sekam, after which it was cremated. Funeral and mourning rites were observed for the image for a whole year. The horror of it! The child had to accept the grass image of a ghost in place of a living person, at the most intimate moment of the wedding ceremony. I think the main character in my play bore a certain likeness to this child widow. She lived till she was very old.

Seeking an heir, a sixty-four-year-old namboodiri married an eighteen year old as his fourth wife. He died soon after. I met her while she was wandering in the Guruvayur and Thripprangot temples, chanting prayers and singing bhajans, a victim of hysteria. When she knew that I was an anterjanam who had abandoned seclusion, she spat at me, went into her room, and slammed the door on my face. I have many sad memories like this one.

A middle-aged woman whom we called "the muthassi from the north," lived with one of my relatives. When she was a child, her mother had been cast out of the community, and the *tarawad* had been ruined by the expenses incurred for the smartavicharam.[6] The daughter was ten years old at the time. She had to go to south Malabar to seek refuge in a wealthy *illam*, where she lived till she was twenty. She learned *kaikottikkali* and music and grew to be a good-looking young woman. A sixty-year-old namboodiri, who had come to the region for a group prayer session, saw her, and was prepared to marry her without a dowry. He hoped that his bride, who was young enough to be his granddaughter, would give him a son to perform his funeral rites. But this did not happen; he died soon after the marriage. The muthassi used to tell us about her mother, who had been cast out because she was suspected of being involved with a young boy whose *upanayanam* had just been performed. She told us that her mother had been taken away by mapillas who had treated her cruelly.

It was this muthassi who first told me the story of Kuriyedathu Tatri. I did not understand it fully at the time. Muthassi whispered it to me, afraid to speak aloud. Poor woman, everyone treated her as if she were mad.

There were a handful of women who had been widowed early in life in my own illam. Three of them were very old. One had two daughters who became widows before they were eighteen, and came back home. Then, there was my grandfather's sister, who had been married to an old man because they said it was difficult to find a younger man whose horoscope matched her unlucky one. She had a younger sister who was also a widow and who lived with her son in her own house.

I heard a story far sadder than all these when I was a little older. It had happened three generations before mine. I knew a muthassi who had been implicated in it. It was brought to light when there was trouble in our family and an *ashtamangalya prasnam* was conducted to find out what was wrong. Puliyoor Purushothaman Namboodiri who was in charge of the prasnam said that there was a soul wandering restlessly around the house, crying, "Narayana, Parameswara," and that it had to be appeased.

This troubled soul was that of a woman who had been the only sister of four brothers. She was widowed when young and since she had no children the brothers had brought her home. She was a woman of great authority and ruled the household with a firm hand. Her brothers' fortunes prospered under her diligent attention. Frugal to a fault, she would not allow the smallest morsel to be wasted.

Naturally, her brothers' wives detested her, and there were quarrels among them all the time. The brothers did not have the courage to defy someone who had cared for them like a mother, but they longed to have peace in the house. One day, one of the sisters-in-law made a trivial mistake while doing her kitchen chores. The sister slapped her with the hand she had been eating with. The younger one hit back, and a fight started. Another sister-in-law, who was sharp-witted enough to be able to seize the opportunity, said, "You don't have any rights in this house; the tarawad and the property belong to us. Go and live in your husband's household and manage its affairs if you want to, that's where you belong, after all."

She was stunned. She had never expected this of her sisters-in-law. She could not accept the idea that her brothers and the tarawad she had served so devotedly could reject her. The blow shattered her completely. She went to her eldest brother, who had overheard the entire quarrel, hoping he would intervene on her behalf. But all he said was, "If you continue to fight with each other, I'll go away somewhere. I want to be left in peace."

Muthassi said, "In that case, it is I who should go away, not you. I'll leave at once, and you can all be happy."

I often think I have inherited the old muthassi's obstinacy. She took her umbrella and shawl and went away immediately. No one called her back, not even her brothers. She looked back repeatedly till the gates shut behind her. Walls about half a mile long surrounded the house, forming a high-walled square around it. There were four gates, one in each wall. Once they were locked at dusk, no one could enter. Muthassi walked till she came to a canal. There was not enough water in it to drown herself, nor did she have a rope to hang herself with. She pondered all night. Her anger cooled by early morning. She came back to the house and knocked at the gate, but no one came to open it. She went around the house many times, calling, "Narayana! Parameswara!" The sisters-in-law sent a servant to say that an anterjanam who had left the house without a companion could not be admitted inside again. She had been cast out.

Muthassi took a decision and went away. She spent the rest of her life wandering around the village. She lived on the tender coconuts and bananas that people gave her. She never cast away her umbrella and never once entered anyone's house. Finally, the sixty-year-old woman, who had once been the head of the well-known Kottavattath Illam, died on the roadside. Or maybe she killed herself. No one was certain how she died.

No one had ever talked of her until the prasnam was done, perhaps because the family had a sense of guilt. I know that my father must have invoked her spirit into an image made of gold and performed the necessary rituals for the peace of her soul. Sometimes I feel that I have taken this task upon myself and that I have inherited her soul. Have I inherited her obstinacy too, and her capacity for renunciation? I feel that talking openly about this unpleasant story is part of a purificatory ritual and that it will cleanse us of the sin we committed in the past, make us pure and whole again. Bhagiratha once brought the Ganga to earth in order to absolve his ancestors of their sins. A similar process of purification has begun in literature too, and my recounting of these widows' stories is part of this great movement.

1967

NOTES

1. See Introduction, pp.xviii–xix.
2. A namboodiri of progressive views, also a playwright.
3. A society for social reform. See Introduction, p.xviii.
4. A society for social reform. See Introduction, p.xx.
5. Shantadevi (1893–1984) wrote short stories in Bengali. Sitadevi (1895–1974) wrote novels in Bengali. Their father, Ramananda Chattopadhyay was the editor of *Modern Review*, an English literary journal.
6. See Introduction, p.xxii.

Sesame Seeds, Flowers, Water

ELLUM POOVUM NEERUM   20

AMME! I HAVE come back. It is your second death anniversary today. The handful of sacrificial rice I hold in my hand was invoked from the heavens into the sacred tree and then into this darbha grass. I mix it with sesame seeds, flowers, and water and offer it to you. I pick up some more sesame seeds and flowers, then water and sandalwood paste. Will you accept this offering? For we have nothing else to give you now.

Have we really nothing else to give? I have thought about this ever since the day you left us. What if I pour all my memories into this offering of sesame seeds and water . . . ? Have you really left us, Amme . . . ? I feel you are always with us now. When you were alive, I did many things of which you disapproved, certain that you would forgive me. But now I pause before I do or say anything and ask myself: Would you have condoned this, could you have borne it? And so, Amme, I have at last become the kind of daughter you wanted me to be.

I often wanted to write about you. Would you have liked me to? You had kept the article and the poem I had written about Achan with such care, I found them in the sheaf of papers you handed over to me at the end. My horoscope was there too, and a notebook that contained pieces I had written as a child. I hope you will forgive my temerity—among the papers that I have collected to hand over to my children and grandchildren, I want to include this article, in which I recall you with deep emotion.

Is it possible to write about you? No, not really. This is not because I consider it difficult to express the greatness of motherhood. I think that era is over, and motherhood is no longer held in high esteem. There are mothers who behave as if their children were mistakes that they should not have made. Still, everyone has a mother, for the age of test-tube babies has not yet arrived. There are all kinds of mothers, from those who love and chastise their children to those who expect to be compensated for the agony of childbirth. Motherhood is an eternal truth, and also an ordinary occurrence. Why then should a sixty-four-year-old woman like me mourn a mother who was over eighty when she died? I do not merely mourn you, Amme. I think, and remember, and the memories go back over six decades. I put them down here, Amme, as they spill out of my mind—for your daughter has this unfortunate habit of wanting to record everything she thinks and feels, since she happens to be a writer. I know you cannot read this with your mortal eyes. But I am certain that you will understand why I have to do this. After all, you told me yourself once that death opens the doors to all realms of knowledge.

I know of the deep emotional bond that exists between a mother and a child, even while the child is in the womb, for I am myself a mother of eight. We look forward to our children with intense hope and longing, and communicate with them powerfully at many levels—through contemplation, sight, touch, and the processes of thought. They claim us totally. We live in a state of being dominated by prayer and hope, almost like penance. Even when a woman conceives after having decided to have no more children, the baby begins to enchant the mother once it quickens in the womb. I was not your eldest child, Amme. But since I was born after you had lost two babies, I became dearer to you than if I had been your first. You always told me that the sex of the baby you carried within you never troubled you and that you did not care whether it was a boy or a girl, even when you ate the butter blessed in the temple, or chanted the special prayers that would ensure you bore a son.

You wanted a baby so that you could be a mother, that was all. You wanted the child to live, to be intelligent. That is all you asked for when you prostrated yourself before the Devi, half an hour before the baby was born.

And so you had a child, a girl. She was not as fair-skinned as you, nor was she pretty. But she tried very hard to be clean and presentable. Although I did not fulfill many of your prayers and hopes, I did give you satisfaction in one respect: I was intelligent, and you always said I had a prodigious memory. If I was told to learn four verses from the *Manipravalam*,[1] I learned and recited about fifteen. I learned everything you taught me, Amme, and this is still the basis of all I know (none of the bits of useless knowledge I gathered stayed with me). When I was a child, we used to recite akshara slokams[2] and samasyas[3] to each other. Whenever you told me a story, you asked me to repeat it to you. But you never imagined, even in your dreams, that I would become a writer, nor did you think of making me one.

All your life, you were afraid of other people, of what they would think or say. It made you very sad when I said it did not matter what they said or thought. But you were never afraid of imparting knowledge to me. My childhood companions were the books you gave me, the newspapers and magazines you filed away for me: *Bhashaposhini, Lakshmi Bai, Rasikaraniani, Atmaposhini*.[4] You arranged them in meticulous order, from the earliest issues. You even kept issues of *Swadeshabhimani*[5] for me because it was the paper that sparked a revolution in your youth. Its courageous editor and his family were held in great respect because they had opposed the government fearlessly and been punished for it. Indeed, the matter was discussed so passionately at home that your three-year-old daughter was heard to exclaim, "What a pity the editor was exiled!" You kept copies of prohibited books like *Parappuram* and *Udayabhanu*[6] for me until I was old enough to read them. Was it because your daughter had access to such books that she later walked so easily on dangerous terrain and became a rebel?

You talked to me about Sita and Savitri, Yashoda and Shilavathi.[7]

We played in the forest with the little Krishna and the incidents of the *Manipravalam* filled my thoughts. Dreams, imagination, and expression were my world. I did not even recognize the occasional assaults reality made on that enchanted world for what they were.

As I grew up, I also watched you tremble in fear. Your very nature was to be frightened of "don'ts." I had long, thick hair like yours. I remember how sad you were that you could not weave jasmines and roses into my braid. In those days, it was a great sin for an unmarried namboodiri girl even to think of wearing fragrant flowers in her hair. Only her husband could put flowers in her hair, on the fourth day of the wedding, when they were alone together for the first time.

Tradition dominated you and you were terrified of calumny. You were afraid of the disapproval of your elders and teachers. I wore a skirt and blouse at home, but you made me take them off when we visited my uncle's house and insisted that I wear only a palm-leaf *konam* and a fine *mundu*, because you feared the grandmothers. You longed to send me to school, but could not. When your grandfather's brother was alive, he had sent you to school. No one had ever dared oppose him, for he was a powerful person with the authority to function as a *smartan* or a *vaidikan*. However, the school you went to was reserved for upper-caste children, in the precincts of the temple. Life was very different for your daughter, who was born in this forest fortress and who had to spend her life within it.

Every day, when my lessons were over, I came to you. We had only each other for company: me for you and you for me. Do you remember one of the amusing games we used to play? You recited a stanza and I had to guess the poet from its style. Then I would recite something and you would guess who had written it. And so they all joined us in our room: Venmani, Sivolli, Oravankara, Naduvam, Kunhukuttam, Ulloor, Vallathol.[8] I recognized most of the poets from the nature of the poem. You sometimes recited one of your own verses, or one of Achan's, and I did not guess correctly. So the days went by.

Then Muthassan died. Achan became the head of the household. When Muthassi died, you became the head of the household. When I think of it now, I want to laugh and cry at the same time— how could a timid, submissive, docile woman like you command a huge extended family like ours, with its innumerable servants, guests, and relatives? It was an unbearably sad situation for you. You had to cook and serve two or three *paras* of rice at every meal. No one was allowed to enter the kitchen except you. And if you left it, you could only go as far as the room of the deities. And of course there were babies every year. Even with a child in the womb and another at your breast, you worked tirelessly.

Our ways separated eventually. You went to the kitchen and I to the reading room. My reading material changed. I read day and night, pondered, dreamed. For the first time, our opinions began to differ. Over the next few years, you did not understand me, nor I you. I had the courage to rebel against the customs you feared. Even if you broke with tradition without meaning to, you trembled for the consequences. Do you remember how you screamed and ran away, the day you almost collided with the priest?

You had to rush all the time from the kitchen to the *nalukettu* in the course of your housework, a distance of about a furlong. One day, Kittan Potti entered with the rice from the *naivedyam* and, in your hurry, you almost ran into him. Both of you were terrified. Hardly aware of what you did, you screamed, "Ayyo—" and ran away. You were worried. Had a man other than your husband touched you? Had he seen your face? That agonized "Ayyo" was part of you.

You liked me to write, but I was careful never to show you what I wrote because I was convinced that I was doing something wrong. And I was worried that you would not like the things I wrote about. Once, the teacher who coached me at home slapped me because my sums were wrong. He then discovered a heap of poems I had written. After Achan and his brothers laughed over them, they gave them to you. You kept them under your mattress, to read them later. I hunted them out and burned them. You said sadly to me, "So many people read them, and you still wanted to hide them from me." I thought the whole world was my enemy. Whenever my opinions differed from yours, I was careful to keep the fact secret from you. I could not help it, Amme! I wanted another sort of life, with more freedom. I longed to move from the shade of the *anterjanam's* umbrella into the bright sunlight. You must have grieved very deeply when I finally did so, you, who screamed because Kittan Potti almost touched you! What hurt you most of all must have been my insistence on doing what I wanted to do, regardless of what others thought.

I often think of what one of the well-known writers of the younger generation said: "Whenever I see my mother look as bewildered as a doe that has given birth to a monkey, it makes me laugh."[9] I cannot help it, Amme, the laughter is part of the dilemma I find myself in.

I remember the blend of shyness and pain with which you posed for a photograph when Achan dragged you to attend a meeting of the anterjanam's association. When Achan broke your bell metal bangles to give you golden ones instead, you sobbed uncontrollably, as if he had broken your mangalyasutram.[10] That day, you did not eat till he gave you permission to wear a bell metal bangle with each of your gold ones.

I remember how you went to Kollam with Achan when he was sick, in a closely curtained car, and how, when you arrived there, you jumped into a well to have a dip because you believed you had been polluted by the journey. Tanks or wells were all the same to you—you were called a water creature when you were a child.

The day I abandoned the system of seclusion, you beat your head and wept. You lamented as if your daughter had died, or been cast out . . .

So many memories stab my heart. Slowly, you became used to it all, and you came to terms with the times you lived in. You did many things that you once thought were sins. Once you even said to me, "I hurt you so much that day, I believed I was concerned about what was good for you. It doesn't matter, everyone is happy now." It doesn't matter, Amme. I hurt you very much too, and both of us shared the pain. And I think I was not hurt as deeply as you were. What matters is that we have the satisfaction that we achieved Sree Narayana Guru's ideal: "What you do for your own happiness should ultimately make everyone happy."

After Achan died, you lived like an ascetic, and now your mind was entirely on your children. Eventually, all human beings became your children. Your affection flowed equally over animals and birds, trees, and creepers. You would often give the rice served on your plate to someone whom you thought was hungrier than you, and starve. You would tell us that it was against the rules of a fast to cook and eat again. When I was a child, I saw you observe five consecutive days of fasting because they happened to fall in a row —Monday, Ekadashi, Pradosham, full moon, and Sivaratri, in that order. On all those days, you cooked and served the usual three paras of rice. All sorts of people enjoyed your hospitality—fugitives, escaped convicts, high officials, and representatives of the people, the rich and the poor. The local schoolchildren wept bitterly when they heard of your death, and someone remarked, "Our 'care center' is gone."

I wanted some of your poems to be published for my sashtiab-dapurthi, or sixtieth birthday. By that time, many of the pieces you had composed as a child had disappeared. Poems were for you flowers for the prayers that blossomed everyday. Poems of praise occurred to you when you stood before the deity for your daily worship, with your eyes closed. You forgot some of these verses later, others stayed in your memory. Many were in praise of the deities—Kasi Vishwanathan, Annapurna, Rama; but they were not only on devotional subjects. You wrote a hymn that extolled the value of principles that went beyond religion and caste in your eighty-second year, and even recorded it for us.

You were born in the month of Medam, when the star Rohini coincided with Akshaya Triteeya.[11] We completed the last day of that year's Saptaham in time for your sathabhishekam.[12] When we all sat together that day, four full generations—you, your children, your grandchildren, and your great-grandchildren—I suddenly noticed a difference in you that made me want to weep. There was an expression I could not define, in those eyes that had seen a thousand full moons. You seemed to have gone away from this world, to be beyond joys and sorrows. You said to us: "Enough. No more. Let's stop now."

Yes, it was true, you were ready to die. There is for death, as for birth, a state of ripeness, of maturity of age and experience. I agree that it is best for oneself and for others to die at that stage of life, and that was what you wanted. Why, then, did you force yourself to survive a whole week on a few drops of *thirtham,* denying yourself all food, without letting any of us know? You had a problem with your heart, and you had already become so weak physically. You were certain that you would die without falling ill, because you had never sinned. You had often told us that disease was a consequence of sin! We tried to argue, to tell you that Sri Ramakrishna Paramahamsa, Ramana Maharshi, and other holy men like them had fallen ill during their lives and submitted themselves to medical treatment. And you had often said that the body is the first entity to which one owes a duty.

In the end you allowed modern medicine and its needles to inject new life into your veins. Meanwhile, you meditated on the infinite, the great universal power and, oblivious to physical exigencies, you lay as light and weightless as a sliver of rust floating upon water. It was as if you slipped back into your childhood in the month that remained. You told us so many stories of that time, about your grandfather's brothers, who were all scholars and poets, one of whom had received the Veerashrinkhala[13] from the maharaja. About the poems that one of the most learned amongst them wanted to teach his disciples, which you learned and could recite before they did, and how you were given a gold-bordered saree as a prize. About how your father married your mother—he came to your sister's wedding as the bridegroom's companion, heard a young girl sing somewhere in the inner rooms of the house and was enchanted by her voice. So he found out who she was and married her. You told us about all the poems that you and your friends wrote and recited, and about your childhood friend, Lakshmikutty Varasyar, the mother of Madassery Madhava Variar.

It shocked the doctor when you told him that it was really best for him to administer drugs that would ensure quick death for bodies that were wasted with age and disease.

You told me that the tulasi branches you had collected over the years and stored in the attic should be used to make your funeral pyre. The old box that had once held palm-leaf manuscripts was filled with blocks of sandalwood for the same purpose. You had stored enough Ganga water too, for the last ritual bath. You wanted everything finished as quickly as possible. You told me I was the only person who would have to cope with the loss of a mother, referring perhaps to the commonly accepted notion that both daughter and daughter-in-law are equally related to a mother. After speaking to me of all these things, you said, "Go now. We will meet again if we are destined to, when my time comes." And you allowed me to leave.

What is this thing called destiny, Amme? How is it decided? Tell me! What power brought me the news, to a place nearly one hundred and twenty-five miles away from where you were, at one o'clock on the night of 16 October 1971? Someone told me later that you called out to me at the very moment when I knew. I started by car before daybreak, and rushed to you. When I arrived, you had had your bath and drunk your *kanji*. You looked very happy when I saw you, with your hand resting on your great-grandson's head in blessing. I said, "Amme, I am here."

"Good! I knew you would come. I have so much to tell you. But I am so tired. I have finished now with this life. I have promised the Devi that I will offer her *payasam* made with five measures of milk if she grants me a quick death. You must make her that offering. And you must give Kali a mundu."

You looked at your son-in-law and said, "I will die today or tomorrow. Let her stay with me till then."

You died that day. I promise to be born as your daughter again in my next life, Amme, to listen to all that you have to tell me. But will I have the good fortune to be born again as your daughter, Amme? Will you have to be born again at all, Amme? I know that you are going to be one with the Great Mother, just as you wished. Give me the vision to look at that Mother as my own, through all my successive lives.

Your lips murmured Bhagavan's name and your fingers moved ceaselessly to count the number of times you said it. You were quite conscious. You were radiant with an inner light. Then you opened your eyes, at five in the evening, and asked what time it was. You told me to open all the doors, light the lamps, and lay you down on the floor. The light of the setting sun suffused the room. Even so, Amme, I did not understand. Someone had brought me an issue of the *Malayalanadu* magazine that carried

Madhavikkutty's autobiography.[14] It lay on my lap as I looked at you. Suddenly, the horizon rumbled and the earth pitched around me. I have a heart ailment, and I had traveled a long distance. What did you murmur, was it, "water," or "Narayana?" You swallowed a mouthful of Ganga water, shuddered, and drew a deep breath. Then there was utter quiet.

People began to gather. Telegrams were dispatched, cars drove up to the house. What had to happen had happened. The children had one more responsibility—performing the funeral rites. When I sat at the feet of your still body, wrapped in an unbleached mundu, I felt nothing. I did not want to cry, or sigh, or even pray. I felt numbed, beyond joy and sorrow, caught in the kind of cosmic stillness that marks the end of a *yuga* or an era. At the height of deep emotion there is a feeling of utter emptiness.

Was it only my physical weakness that had led me to imagine the roaring of the air around me? Was it my blood pressure? Or was it what you used to tell me it was, Amme, did the chariots of the divine messengers come to take you? Who knows! We can only guess the truth. The moment when God becomes a human being and then becomes God once again, that is the moment of death. All human beings are a part of God. But can all human beings enter into God? Can the human soul (or human reality), which has moved from life in the world to the life beyond, come back? I don't want to think about it any more, Amme! I will never be able to find an answer, so let this question, which has been asked from the beginning of time, remain a question.

Before I end this piece, however, I must describe a very worldly incident that took place that night. Kali was a poor harijan who still believed in old traditions. Although the laws of untouchability had been abolished, she hesitated to come anywhere near us. She would stand in the courtyard, you would be in the veranda, and you would both talk for hours at this distance from each other. You had a very special affection for her—perhaps becaue she was the same age as the first baby you lost. Shaken by the news of your death, she rushed into the nalukettu, crying loudly, "My *thampuratti*, I've lost everything I had!" She beat her head, fell senseless at the feet of the body and began to roll on the ground. Her relatives came and carried her away. What was the nature of Kali's bond with us? Is it amongst people like her that you will be born again?

I gave the Devi the offering of milk payasam that you had promised her, to ensure a quick death for yourself, Amme! And I gave Kali her mundu too.

An era ended with you, Amme. I don't think that I can ever be its representative, for each generation has its own individual reality. And yet, I too am a link in the hereditary chain of universal motherhood, which was established from the beginning of time and which reached down to you, Amme. Its nature has permeated my blood vessels, my senses, my life. I know that motherhood is a universal truth. And so let me place this offering of sesame seeds, flowers, and water here with the courage and conviction that I have understood this truth, for the souls of all the mothers that have died, on behalf of all the mothers who are alive. Come, in the form of my mother, and receive it!

1973

NOTES

1. The *Sri Krishna Charitram* (The Story of Krishna) by Kunchan Nambiar. Its language is also called Manipravalam: a mixture of Sanskrit and Malayalam, from "mani," "ruby" in Malayalam, and "pravalam," "coral" in Sanskrit.
2. A competition in which verses are recited in Sanskrit or in Malayalam; the first participant chants a verse and the second one has to follow with a verse that begins with the first letter of the third line of the quatrain just chanted. Competitors who fail to come up with a verse are disqualified.
3. A recitation competition; the fourth line of a quatrain is given and the other three have to be recited.
4. Founded in 1892, 1905, 1905 and 1910 (in order of appearance); these are magazines that were widely read when Lalithambika Antherjanam was growing up.

5. A newspaper that became famous when K. Ramakrishna Pillai (1978–1916) became its editor in 1906. He was exiled from Travancore for writing against the government in 1911, his press was confiscated and the newspaper folded up.
6. Published in 1890 and in 1904, these are political novels by Narayana Kurukkal (1861–1948). Ramakrishna Pillai (see n.5) was involved in their publication.
7. Ideal women from the Hindu epics who are also venerated.
8. All poets; the Venmani school of the late nineteenth-century poets broke the domination of Sanskrit and made Malayalam poetry popular. The last two poets mentioned are of the twentieth century.
9. Kamala Das, the well-known writer who writes in both Malayalam and English.
10. The necklace tied round the bride's neck during the marriage ceremony.
11. The third day of the month of Vaisaka (Edavam in the Malayalam calendar), considered to be very auspicious.
12. The eighty-fourth birthday, a very important occasion because the celebrant has witnessed a thousand full moons.
13. A gold chain awarded by the maharaja in return for bravery.
14. *My Story* by Kamala Das, who writes in Malayalam as Madhavikkutty (see also n.9).

Glossary

abhishekam anointing of the deity with rosewater, oil, ghee, milk, or honey
ahimsa nonviolence, the Jain and Buddhist ideal, taught and practised in the nationalist movement by Mahatma Gandhi
Ambika one of the names of the Goddess Parvathi
anchampura a building outside the main living quarters, where the accused in a smartavicharam was kept in isolation
angavastram a short piece of cloth worn over the shoulder by men
Annapurna/Annapuneswari the Devi in the form of the generous giver
antahpuram the inner rooms to which women were confined
anterjanam she who lives inside: a synonym for a namboodiri woman
ashtamangalyam eight auspicious objects arranged on a bronze or silver platter and used on special occasions such as the welcoming of a bride. A well-known verse lists them as ululations, mirror, lamp, ten sacred flowers, newly washed cloth, paddy rice, a beautiful woman and gold; there is some variation in practice. For obvious reasons, kohl replaces the woman.
ashtamangalya prasnam ritual performed to find out why a family has suffered a misfortune, in which the eight auspicious objects are used
ashtapadi the songs of Jayadeva's *Gita Govinda*
Bhagavatham a Puranam on the incarnations of Vishnu, especially Krishna
bhakta one who follows the path of devotion, bhakti
Brindavanam a forest on the banks of the Kalindi River where Krishna spent his youth as a cowherd
chunam lime paste that is spread on betel leaves
Ekadashi the eleventh day after the new moon and the full moon; a day of fasting for women.

garbhagriha sanctum sanctorum of the temple
gopi/gopika cowherd woman who participates in Krishna's divine play
Guruvayurappan the deity of the Guruvayur temple, Krishna
homakundam the pit where the fire for the homam is lit
homam the offering made to the fire-god, Agni
illam a namboodiri landlord's household, commonly built as a rectangle
   enclosing an inner courtyard
japamala a chain of beads, used when saying prayers
kadukka nuts bitter-tasting nuts with medicinal value
kafir term used by Muslims to refer to non-Muslims
kaikottikkali a dance done by women. They sing and dance in a circle
kaliyuga the fourth and last era of the world, filled with violence and god-
   lessness
kanji rice served with the water in which it has been cooked
karyasthan a steward or manager of a large estate
khadar material made with yarn that is handspun; khadi
kindi vessel made of copper, bell metal, or silver with a spout
konam a long piece of material used to cover the genitals; made from cloth
   or from a tender palm spathe
kunukku very long dangling earrings
mapilla a Kerala Muslim
Meera sixteenth-century Rajput princess who forsook her royal role to devote her life to Krishna
mleccha term used by upper-caste Hindus to refer to non-Hindus
moksha Hindu belief in the deliverance from the cycle of birth, death, and
   rebirth; of the soul merging with God
mundu an ankle-length piece of cloth worn round the waist by men and
   women in Kerala
naivedyam food offerings to the deity, usually rice and payasam
nalukettu a house built around a rectangular courtyard open to the sky;
   the word also refers to the courtyard itself.
Onam festival celebrated over ten days in August–September
pandal a temporary structure, like a large tent or even a building, made
   of bamboo or wood
para an approximately 12 kg measure of paddy or rice
payasam a sweet made with milk, sugar, and rice
pradakshinam circumambulation of a temple in clockwise direction
Pradosham the twelfth day after the new moon and the full moon when
   women fast
prasadam food, flowers and sandalwood paste offered to a deity that are
   distributed among devotees
prathaman a festive sweet made with mashed bananas or jackfruit, or mashed
   lentils, cooked with molasses and coconut milk

rasa essence; an aesthetic theory based on the nine rasas or moods in art
rudraksha a dried fruit, used to make japamalas
saptaham the reading of a religious text, usually of the Bhagavatham, over
   seven days
shraddha annual rites for the dead
sinduram a red powder used by married women to make a mark on their
   forehead
smartan a brahmin who acts as a judge in a smartavicharam, the trial of
   namboodiri women accused of having illicit relationships or of having
   flouted caste norms
sreekovil the sanctum sanctorum of a temple
swadeshi made in one's own country; the conscious decision to boycott
   British manufactured goods during the nationalist movement
tamboolam betel leaves smeared with areca nuts and chunam
tarawad the extended namboodiri/nair household; in the case of nairs, of
   matrilineal descent
thali mangalyasutram, the gold pendant on a yellow or white thread, tied
   around the bride's neck at marriage and removed when she is widowed
thampuran a respectful form of address meaning "lord," often used for the
   male head of an estate or of a powerful family
thampuratti a respectful form of address for the mistress of a household
thevaram the daily worship of the deity
thilakam a mark made with vermilion powder on their foreheads by married
   women
thirtham sacred water that has been used for the abhishekam that is offered to worshippers
thirumanassu/thirumeni a respectful form of addresss for brahmins and
   royalty
trimadhuram prasadam made with bananas, molasses, and honey
upanayanam the initiation ceremony that gives a brahmin boy, the right
   to study the Vedas and wear the sacred thread
Vadakkunnathan Siva, the deity of the temple at Thrissur
vadikkini a room in the northern wing of the nalukettu, adjacent to the
   kitchen to which women have free access
vaidikan a scholar of the Vedas, who supervises the rituals
vaidyan a practitioner of indigenous medicine
vedantin one who has studied the Vedanta
vibhuti holy ashes, smeared by worshippers on their foreheads
vidyarambham the ceremony performed when a child is first taught the
   letters of the alphabet
Vishu the Malayalam New Year, the first day of the month of Medam
   (April–May)

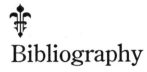

Bibliography

BOOKS BY LALITHAMBIKA ANTHERJANAM

S H O R T   S T O R I E S

Adyathe Kathakal, 1937
Moodupadathil, 1946
Thakarna Talamura, 1949
Kalathinde Edukal, 1950
Kilivathaliloote, 1950
Koddumkattil Ninnu, 1951
Kannirinte Punjiri, nd
Irupathu Varshathinu Sesham, 1956
Agnipushpangal, 1960
Satyathinte Swaram, 1968
Viswaroopam, 1971
Ishtadevata, 1971
Thiranjedutha Kathakal, 1966
Dhirendu Majumdarude Amma, 1973
Pavitramothiram, 1979

P O E M S

Onakkazhcha, nd
Lalithanjali, 1939
Sharana Manjari, nd
Bhava Deepti, nd
Nishabda Sangeetham, nd

Oru Pottichiri, 1958
Aayirathiri (Selected Poems), 1969

FOR CHILDREN

Kunjomana, nd
Gosi Paranja Katha, nd
Thenthullikal, 1968
Grama Balika, 1951

NOVEL

Agnisakshi, 1976

ESSAY

Sita Muthal Satyavathi Vare, 1972

AUTOBIOGRAPHY

Atmakathakkoru Amukkham (Preface for an Autobiography). Thrissur:
Current Books, 1979

SELECTED READINGS

Alexander, Meena, "Outcaste Power: Ritual Displacement and Virile Maternity in Indian Women Writers." *Economic and Political Weekly* 24, 7
(1989): 367-372.
George, K. M., ed., *Inner Spaces: Malayalam Stories by Women*. Delhi:
Kali for Women, 1995.
James, Jancy, "Feminism as Social Commitment: The Case of Lalitham-
bika Antharjanam." *Indian Literature* 173 (May-June 1996).
M. Leelavathi, *M. Leelavathi: Kavyarathi*. Thrissur: National Book Stall,
1993.
Menon, Dilip, *Caste, Nationalism and Communism in South India: Mala-
bar, 1900-1948*. Delhi: Oxford University Press, 1994.
Menon, Sridhara, *A Survey of Kerala History*. Chennai: S. Viswanathan,
1988.
N. Krishna Pillai, *Akaporul Thedi*. Thrissur: Sahitya Akademi, 1990.
Paimbilli, Joseph. *Antherjanam: Oru Padanam*. (Festschrift, Antherjanam:
A Study) Ramampuram: Antherjanam Sastiabdapurthi Celebration Com-
mittee, 1969.
Tharu, Susie, and K. Lalita, eds., *Women Writing in India*, 2 vols. New
York: The Feminist Press, 1991, 1993; Delhi: Oxford University Press,
1992, 1994.